GW00507779

Living Through History

INDIAN INDEPENDENCE

STEPHEN ASHTON

Batsford Academic and Educational
London

ACKNOWLEDGMENTS

The Author and Publishers would like to thank the following for their kind permission to reproduce copyright material: Associated Press for figure 57; BBC Hulton Picture Library for figure 58; Lady Birdwood for transcripts from *Plain Tales from the Raj*; Mrs Susan Brown for extracts from *Tea Tales of Assam* by Kenneth Warren and for figures 42, 43 and 44; Cassell for figure 34; Controller of HMSO for extracts from the letters of Lord Irwin (Crown copyright); Irene Edwards for transcripts from *Plain Tales from the Raj*; Faltis Collection, National Archives of India for figure 31; Imperial War Museum for figure 23; India Office Library and Records for figures 1, 3, 4, 5, 6, 7, 8, 9, 15, 16, 17, 18, 21, 22, 24, 25, 26-9, 32, 33, 35, 37, 38, 39, 40, 41, 48, 50, 51, 52, 53, 54, 56, 59 and 60; Lady Rosamund Lawrence for figure 36 from *Plain Tales from the Raj*, ed. Charles Allen; Mansell Collection for figure 2; Sir Penderel Moon OBE for transcripts from *Plain Tales from the Raj* and for figures 11, 12, 13 and 14; Nehru Memorial Museum and Library for figure 20; *Punch* Library for figures 10 and 19; Professor Hugh Tinker for figures 45, 46 and 47; Trustees of the Broadlands Archives Settlement for figure 30. The map on page 60 was drawn by R.F. Brien.

Cover illustrations

The colour photograph shows the postage stamp commemorating India's independence on 15 August 1947. The Hindi script reads *Jai Hind*, "Victory to India". The black and white photograph on the left shows Gandhi leaving Viceregal Lodge and the portrait is of Lord Irwin (both courtesy of India Office Library and Records).

Frontispiece

Gandhi and Nehru (left) at a refugee camp in the Punjab, 1947 (India Office Library and Records).

Typeset by Tek-Art Ltd, West Wickham, Kent
Printed in Great Britain by
R.J. Acford Ltd,
Chichester, Sussex
for the publishers
Batsford Academic and Educational,
an imprint of B.T. Batsford Ltd,
4 Fitzhardinge Street
London W1H 0AH

ISBN 0 7134 4774 5

CONTENTS

LIST OF
ILLUSTRATIONS

INDIAN INDEPENDENCE

As long as we rule India, we are the greatest power in the world. If we lose it, we shall drop straightaway to a third-rate power.

So wrote Lord Curzon, Viceroy of India, in 1901. In August 1947 the unthinkable for Curzon happened. The British handed over power to two successor states – India and a new Muslim state of Pakistan. The ending of British rule in India was momentous in itself. It created the world's largest parliamentary democracy and, until the civil war and the emergence of Bangladesh in 1971, the world's largest (in terms of population) Muslim state. But it also had repercussions which extended far beyond the Indian subcontinent. As the first major act of decolonization in Asia by a European power, it marked the beginning of a process whereby European colonial empires, French and Dutch as well as British, began to retreat under pressure from a new wave of Asian nationalism.

This section examines how and why Britain felt obliged to concede independence to India in 1947. Historians have put forward three principal arguments to explain this process: first, the pressure exerted by Indian nationalism; secondly, the changing nature of Britain's interests in India; and, finally, the effects on Britain of the Second World War. We shall look at the significance of each in turn.

Unlike the nationalists in French Indo-China and Dutch Indonesia, the Indian nationalists did not have to fight a prolonged anti-colonial war to gain their freedom. Instead they relied, in the main, on non-violent methods of political protest. The British responded to such protest with repression on the one hand but with reform on the other. Never more than a few thousand amidst a population of nearly 400 million, the British had never ruled India entirely on their own. They always depended on a degree of Indian cooperation and collaboration. To ensure that such cooperation would always be forthcoming, the British were forced to introduce political reforms, to increase the number of Indian officers in the Indian army and to increase the Indian element in the civil services. By the end of the Second World War, there were less than 500 senior British civil servants and only 200 British police in the whole of India.

In an administrative sense, therefore, Indians were virtually running their own country by 1947. But if nationalist pressure brought India that much closer to self-government, it never brought the British to their knees, not even in 1942 when, with the Japanese seemingly poised to invade India from neighbouring Burma, the Indian National Congress attempted to paralyze the administration by launching a "Quit India" movement. Moreover, by the 1940s, the Indian nationalists did not speak with one voice. The Indian National Congress and the All-India Muslim League were united in their demand for independence but divided over the crucial question of how this independence was to be achieved. To argue along these lines is not to belittle the nationalist achievement, nor to overlook the sacrifices which were undoubtedly made. It does, however, suggest that other factors contributed to the British withdrawal.

A further explanation suggests that where once the nature of Britain's interests in India made British rule absolutely vital, this was perhaps no longer the case by the 1940s. During the imperial heyday at the turn of the century, the British had governed India in order to acquire maximum profit at minimum expense. Questions of prestige apart, India

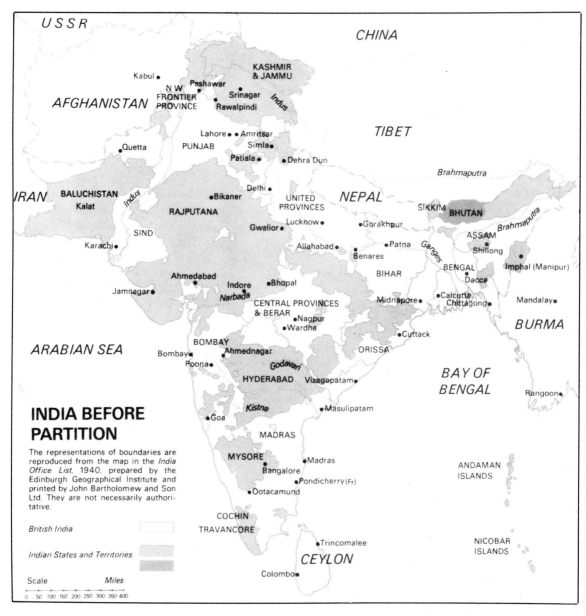

1 India before partition.

had been important to Britain for two reasons. First she was an important source for raw materials and a major market for British manufactures, especially cotton textiles; secondly, she provided Britain with enormous military resources. British troops stationed in India and the Indian army itself were both paid for by the Indian tax-payer. The Indian army, the largest volunteer army anywhere in the world, provided the means whereby the British Empire could expand and defend its

influence from the Middle East to the Pacific. In 1882 Lord Salisbury likened India to "an English barrack in the Oriental Seas from which we may draw any number of troops without paying for them".

By the mid-twentieth century, however, the pattern of Britain's relationship with India had begun to change. India was still an important market for British goods but no longer a vital one. The textile industry carried less weight in Britain's domestic economy. New industries, such as chemicals and engineering, found little outlet in India, nor did they depend on India for raw materials.

British business interests in India, particularly in tea and jute, could be maintained through agreement with the government of an independent India. But the most significant change concerned the Indian army. As it became more sensitive about Indian opinion on the question of how money should be spent, the British government in India found it increasingly difficult to muster the resources needed to keep the Indian army abreast of technological change. In an age of the tank and the aeroplane, the Indian army began to seem static and cumbersome. Britain was deeply indebted to the Indian army. In recognition of the fact that India had provided over one million troops during the First World War and over two million during the Second, the British Chiefs of Staff observed in 1946:

From the military point of view one of India's most important assets is an almost inexhaustable supply of manpower. . . . Without this help it would have been difficult to have won the last two wars.

In the long-term, however, without the modernization which Britain could ill-afford,

2 Imperial splendour: the princes' procession at the Delhi Durbar, 1903. The Durbar was organized by the Viceroy, Lord Curzon, to celebrate the coronation in 1902 of the King-Emperor, Edward VII.

the Indian army would not be of much use outside India. This did not mean that India had ceased to be a military asset: she was still important to Britain in a strategic sense. She provided the means whereby Britain could patrol the Indian Ocean and protect the oil from the Persian Gulf, and also maintain air and sea communications with Africa and Arabia on the one side and Australia and the Far East on the other. For these reasons the Chiefs of Staff wanted to negotiate a defence treaty with the new Indian government when India became independent. They envisaged that such a treaty would provide Britain, not only with military bases in India, but also with continued access to India's industrial resources and manpower. These demands were totally unrealistic and, for political reasons, they were never in fact placed before the new Indian government. They would most certainly have been rejected. India's new leaders were not prepared to allow themselves

to be exploited in this way by their former colonial masters.

Nationalist agitation in India created the necessary climate for India's independence. Britain's belief, however misguided from a military point of view, that it could safeguard its interests when India became independent, provided at least one important motive. But the actual timing of Britain's departure from India in 1947 was largely determined by changes brought about by the Second World War. Britain emerged in 1945 exhilerated by victory but economically exhausted and militarily vulnerable. If serious unrest were

3 "An English barrack in the Oriental Seas": Indian cavalry regiment in France during the First World War.

4 End of Empire. Lord Mountbatten, the last Viceroy, with, on his right, Jawaharlal Nehru, the Congress leader, and, on his left, Mahomed Ali Jinnah, the leader of the Muslim League, presides over the meeting at Delhi on 2 June 1947 at which the Indian leaders agreed to the partition of India.

now to develop, not only in India, but also in countries such as Burma, Malaya and Palestine, it was doubtful whether Britain had the strength to hold its position. Field Marshal Montgomery expressed the views of the Chiefs of Staff when he observed in September 1946 that they were "approaching the position when we would no longer be able to meet our commitments". The war also brought about a change of government in Britain. In the general election of July 1945 Winston Churchill's Conservatives went down to an unexpected defeat at the hands of Clement Attlee's Labour party. For Churchill, the British Empire in India had always been a source of immense pride. In February 1935 he told the House of Commons:

We have as good a right to be in India as anyone; our Government is incomparably the best Government that India has ever seen or ever will see.

As Britain's war-time Prime Minister, during which time he resisted pressure which came not only from sections of public opinion in Britain but also from his American ally, Churchill continued to pour scorn on the very concept of Indian self-government. His defeat in 1945 thus removed a major obstacle standing in India's way. The Labour Party had always been more sympathetic towards India's nationalist aspirations and went into the election pledged to the early realization of Indian self-government. But the new Labour government was not necessarily against the possession of an overseas empire. It had, for instance, no intention of relinquishing Britain's colonies in tropical Africa where the problem of nationalism did not as yet exist. India, however, was different, as Attlee explained in a letter to Ernest Bevin, the Foreign Secretary, in January 1947:

It has been common ground with all of us who have had to study the Indian problem that there are millions of Indians who do not really wish for a change of government, but they are passive. The active elements in the population, including practically all the educated classes, have become indoctrinated to a greater or lesser extent with nationalism. . . . It would be quite impossible, even if you could find the men, for a few hundred British to administer against the active opposition of the whole of the politically minded of the population.

With a Labour government in Britain, therefore, it was no longer a question of whether Britain would transfer power in India but rather a question of to whom that power should be transferred.

BRITISH OFFICIALS IN INDIA

This section looks at the manner in which the British responded to the demands of the Indian nationalist movement and also at the role of British civilians and military personnel in India. It examines the Indian experiences of three men who occupied different positions within the official British hierarchy: at the top, one of the Viceroys; in the middle, a career civil servant in the Indian Civil Service; and, at the bottom, a soldier in the British army in India.

Lord Mountbatten, the last Viceroy, described the viceroyalty as "the greatest office in the world". Outwardly there was much to be said for this view. The Viceroy presided over an empire larger then the entire continent of Europe without Russia, with a population which was exceeded only by that of China. On state occasions the Viceroy sat on a throne. He had his own bodyguard of scarlet lancers, every bit as splendid as the Household Cavalry which served the monarch in Britain. The Viceroy's salary was twice that of the British Prime Minister. Gandhi saw fit to

5 Letter from the Prime Minister, Clement Attlee, to King George VI recommending that Lord Mountbatten should replace Lord Wavell as the last Viceroy of India. The King's signature of approval is at the top.

10, Downing Street,
Whitehall.

Mr. Attlee, with his humble duty to Your Majesty.

He has kept Your Majesty currently informed of his views on the question of the Viceroyalty of India. There is no statutory term of office for the Viceroy and at the time of appointment, as recorded in Cabinet minutes, Viscount Wavell was only given the indication that the appointment might be for three years in order to leave it open for his resignation to be requested without any sense of disappointment on his part, if the circumstances made it desirable. The three year period ended in June, 1946.

For reasons which Mr. Attlee has explained to Your Majesty, he considers that it will soon be his duty to recommend that Viscount Wavell should be replaced by Viscount Mountbatten. It is not possible at the moment for Mr. Attlee to forecast when this change will take place, but it will probably fall during Your Majesty's visit to the Union of South Africa.

Mr. Attlee ...

10, Downing Street,
Whitehall.

Mr. Attlee trusts that in that event a submission to this effect may be agreeable to Your Majesty, and that he may deal by telegram with any recommendation for honours which it may be desirable to submit.

All of which is submitted by Your Majesty's humble, obedient Servant,

C.R. Attlee.

29th January, 1947.

remind one Viceroy that the Viceroy's salary was over 5000 times India's average income. But despite the splendours of his office, the Viceroy was not an absolute ruler. He was appointed, usually for five years, by the government in London. The speed of twentieth-century communications made it possible for the Secretary of State for India and, through him, the Cabinet as a whole, to keep the Viceroy on a tight rein. Only Mountbatten was given a free hand to make major policy decisions on his own. The Mountbatten viceroyalty, however, was exceptional. Appointed in March 1947, Mountbatten was given 15 months to bring an end to British rule in India, a task which he actually completed in just over four.

The day-to-day administration of India was the responsibility of the Indian Civil Service. Traditionally the ICS was the preserve of Oxbridge graduates with public school backgrounds. The first Indians were appointed to the ICS in the 1860s but aspiring

6 England in India. Viceregal Lodge at Simla in the foothills of the Himalayas was the hot-weather retreat for the Viceroy and his staff.

Indian applicants were handicapped because they had to travel to England to sit the entrance examination. In 1909 there were only 60 Indians in a total cadre of 1142. The pattern of recruitment to the ICS began to change after the First World War and life was made easier for Indian candidates by the introduction in 1921 of a simultaneous entrance examination held in India. Concern over pay and conditions, the prospect of serving under Indian ministers and nationalist agitation in general combined to make it more difficult to attract British recruits. In 1922, concerned to drum up support for the ICS, Lloyd George, the Prime Minister, declared in the House of Commons:

I can see no period when the Indians can dispense with the guidance and assistance of the small nucleus of the British Civil Service of British officials in India. . . . They are the steel frame of the whole structure . . . if you take that steel frame out, the fabric will collapse.

Colonel Wedgwood, the Labour spokesman in the same debate, was no less complimentary about the ICS but rather more prophetic when he declared that "the best of the British officers in India realize that they are doing the finest service to the Mother Country when they assist forward the process of their own extinction".

Underpinning the army of civil servants was the British army itself. A substantial number of British troops had been kept in India after the Great Revolt of 1857 and, although smaller than the Indian army (the fighting strength of the British army in India in 1925 was 57,000 compared with the 140,000 of the Indian army), the British army performed many of the same functions. It guarded India's frontiers and maintained internal security when necessary, and was ultimately responsible for the safety of British civilians in India.

Lord Irwin (1881-1959)

In 1868 a Hindu astrologer told the then Viceroy, Sir John Lawrence, that a descendant of Sir Charles Wood, the first Secretary of State for India, would one day become Viceroy. This prophecy was fulfilled in 1926 when Edward Wood, Sir Charles' grandson, resigned his seat as a Conservative MP in the House of Commons and assumed the title of Lord Irwin to become the sixteenth Viceroy of India.

The appointment came as a surprise, not least to the new Viceroy himself. He had risen rapidly in politics, overcoming the handicap of having been born with no left hand, to achieve Cabinet rank in 1922 at the age of only 41. But, despite his family connection with India and his academic achievement, Irwin was not at all confident. He told his wife that he did not think he was "up to the job". Besides, he was reluctant to be parted from his father, a frail old man of 86, to whom he was devoted. Unaware that the King had put forward his name, Irwin at first declined. It was only the personal intervention of Stanley

7 Lord Irwin in the Star of India robes which he wore when he was sworn in as Viceroy.

Baldwin, the Prime Minister, that persuaded him to change his mind.

Irwin arrived in India at a time of relative political calm. His predecessor, Lord Reading, had borne the brunt of Gandhi's non-cooperation movement between 1920 and 1922. Outbreaks of violence, which culminated in a mob burning to death 22 policemen in their station at Chauri Chaura in the United Provinces, had persuaded Gandhi to call off non-cooperation in February 1922. Gandhi had been arrested and sentenced to six years' imprisonment of which, on the grounds of ill health, he served only two. When he was released in 1924 he stayed out of politics, concentrating instead on schemes for social and economic reform. In his absence, the Indian National Congress lacked both leadership and ideas.

Irwin's views on India reflected the outlook of most British politicians at the time. India, it was said, was not ready for self-government. The Indian nationalists, particularly those who led Congress, were regarded as an educated minority who did not represent the "real India" – the millions of illiterate and uneducated peasants for whose welfare the British considered they had a special responsibility. In November 1927 Irwin informed his father that he had "broken the ice" and met Gandhi. Gandhi put forward the view that Britain had "no moral claim" to be the judge of Indian progress. The Viceroy found his visitor "an interesting personality" but one who was "singularly remote" from practical politics:

8 Lady Irwin. The Viceroy's wife did not always enjoy her official role. She disliked the protocol and felt "like a child caught doing something naughty" when the head of the household found her trying to rearrange the furniture in the drawing room at the Viceroy's Delhi residence.

It was rather like talking to someone who had stepped off one planet on to this for a short visit of a fortnight, and whose whole mental outlook was quite other to that which was regulating most of the affairs on the planet to which he had descended.

Irwin's attitude explained why, in making his first major political decision, he was also responsible for a serious error of judgement. Largely at his insistence, a Commission which was appointed at the end of 1927 to examine the working of the 1919 Government of India Act consisted entirely of representatives from the political parties in Britain. Not a single Indian was appointed. Irwin thought it would be impossible to appoint Indians who would be both acceptable and representative. He knew that his decision would not be popular and that there would be some protest but he hoped that this would soon blow over.

The Viceroy was wrong. Indian leaders regarded the absence of Indians on the Commission as a national insult. When the Commission arrived in India it was greeted by demonstrations, and everywhere it went its

13

proceedings were boycotted by all but a handful of the main political parties. The protests injected new life into Congress. In order to prove that Indians were capable of governing themselves, Congress set up a committee, which produced a report calling for self-government on the basis of Dominion Status. This did not, however, satisfy the younger and more radical members of Congress such as Jawaharlal Nehru and Subhas Chandra Bose. They wanted a clean break and demanded complete independence *outside* the British Empire. The issue threatened to split Congress and so, at the end of 1928, Gandhi emerged from retirement to suggest a compromise: if Dominion Status had not been granted by the end of 1929, Congress would stand for complete independence and start civil disobedience to achieve it.

Aware now of the consequences of his misjudgement, Irwin attempted to make amends. He came back to England on leave in the middle of 1929 and persuaded the Labour government to allow him to make a statement confirming that Dominion Status was the goal of British policy in India and inviting Indian representatives to attend a Round Table Conference in London to discuss the next step forward. Irwin's statement was announced when he arrived back in India in October 1929 but it did not satisfy the radicals in Congress as it did not specify when India would achieve Dominion Status. Gandhi insisted that it should be granted immediately and that the purpose of the conference in London should be to work out the details. To this Irwin would not, indeed could not, agree. At the end of 1929 Congress rejected the conference invitation and opted instead for civil disobedience.

9 Lord and Lady Irwin (seated centre) with their personal staff at Viceregal Lodge, Simla.

Gandhi launched his campaign by defying the Salt Acts. The government had a monopoly over salt manufacture in India. Private salt manufacture was illegal. All Indians used salt and all paid a salt tax. This amounted to four old pence per annum per head – nearly three days' income for the very poor. On 12 March 1930, Gandhi set out to walk 240 miles through Gujarat to the coast at Dandi. He arrived amidst great publicity on 6 April and proceeded to break the law by making salt from sea water on the beach. On 7 April Irwin wrote to his father:

I am anxious to avoid arresting Gandhi if I can do so without letting a "Gandhi legend" establish itself that we are afraid to lay hands on him. This we clearly cannot afford.

The Viceroy regarded the salt march as little more than a publicity stunt and he tried at first to ignore what was happening. But Gandhi had captured the popular imagination and thousands followed his example. Irwin had no option but to order his arrest. Gandhi was detained on 4 May but this did not deter his followers and soon most of the Congress leaders were also in prison. There were outbreaks of violence on both sides as civil disobedience began to spread: eight guards were murdered when an armoury was raided at Chittagong in Bengal and, north of Bombay, hundreds of demonstrators attempting to occupy the Dharsana salt works offered no resistance as they were beaten with truncheons by policemen guarding the factory gates.

At the height of the disturbances, Irwin stood firm. Although a man with deep religious convictions, he had no hesitation in signing the death warrants of those convicted of terrorist murders. But while taking stern measures, Irwin realized that force alone was not enough. However much he disagreed with the aims and methods of Congress, he could not ignore the fact that it was the most important nationalist party. Without its cooperation, any settlement reached at the conference which had assembled in London would almost certainly fail. The Viceroy

CONVERSATION FOR TWO.
Mr. Winston Churchill. "I hope I intrude."

10 Winston Churchill makes known his opposition to the talks which led to the Gandhi-Irwin Pact.

therefore made agreement with Congress his priority. He appealed to Gandhi for peace and then ordered his release from prison in January 1931. On 17 February Gandhi was escorted into the Viceroy's House in New Delhi for the first of a series of meetings with Irwin. The negotiations ended on 5 March with an agreement which became known as the Gandhi-Irwin Pact. Gandhi agreed to call off civil disobedience and to attend a second Round Table Conference in London. In return, Irwin ordered the release of all prisoners who had not been guilty of acts of violence. The agreement was Irwin's last major act as Viceroy. He returned to Britain in April 1931 at the end of his five-year term of office.

The Pact was a victory for common sense, but it proved to be short-lived. Congress radicals thought that Gandhi had given in too easily. In Britain, Conservative politicians were dismayed by what Irwin had done.

Winston Churchill led the chorus of protest, declaring himself outraged by

the nauseating and humiliating spectacle of this one time Inner Temple lawyer, now seditious fakir, striding half-naked up the steps of the Viceroy's palace there to negotiate and parley on equal terms with the representative of the King-Emperor.

Gandhi travelled to Britain in the autumn of 1931 but his presence at the conference table in London failed to produce a political settlement. Civil disobedience was resumed when he returned to India at the end of the year. Irwin's successor, Lord Willingdon, was determined to crush the protest movement. Gandhi and other Congress leaders were re-arrested and Congress itself was outlawed.

Irwin succeeded his father as Lord Halifax in 1934. He served as Foreign Secretary between 1938 and 1940 and then, during the war, as Britain's ambassador in Washington. The European crisis at the end of the Thirties, particularly the Munich settlement with Hitler, has tended to overshadow his role as Viceroy. But India was perhaps the pinnacle of his career. He regarded Churchill's attack on his policy as the product of a mentality which belonged to a bygone age. As he told his father:

I can of course very well understand the attitude of people who would say that it was wholly wrong for the Government to discuss settlement at all until the Congress people had come on their knees petitioning for mercy. The answer to that seems to me to be that it rests upon assumptions that are totally unrelated to fact, and in effect proceeds from an order of ideas which is quite different to the order of ideas on which the whole policy of trying to make India self-governing is necessarily based. That is to say, surely the efforts to make India self-governing – be they wise or unwise – necessarily involve the obtaining of as large a measure of assent as possible in what you do, in order that the process may go on with some degree of smoothness.

For all his differences with Congress, Irwin preferred cooperation to confrontation and he was sincere in his efforts to gain an understanding with its leaders. He earned their admiration and respect. As one of them said, having dealt with many of the Viceroys, Irwin was "the most Christian and the most gentlemanly of them all".

Penderel Moon (b. 1905)

Penderel Moon first thought of joining the Indian Civil Service when he was a senior boy at Winchester public school a few years after the First World War. The school was visited by an outside speaker who painted a very idealistic picture of the life and work of members of the ICS. Particular emphasis was placed on the role of the ICS in teaching Indians how to govern themselves. It was not until later that he discovered that the ICS had been experiencing difficulty securing new recruits and that speakers had been sent round to all the public schools. Moon was, therefore, in his own words, a "victim of propaganda".

When Moon left Winchester he went to Oxford University to finish his education. In 1928 he passed the entrance examination for the ICS and then spent a probationary year in England before proceeding to the Punjab, the province of his choice, in 1929. His probationary year was spent at Oxford learning Urdu (one of the languages spoken in the Punjab) and gaining some familiarity with Indian history and Indian law. Looking back, he considered the year to have been "an atrocious waste of time". He learnt little about the province for which he was destined and wondered why it had not been possible to arrange for an experienced officer who was home on leave to give a lecture to the probationers on the Punjab and the Muslims, Sikhs and Hindus who lived there. He worked hard at Urdu only to find when he arrived in the Punjab that the main language was Punjabi. This meant that when he first presided in court as a magistrate he could not understand a word of what was being said by the uneducated villagers. Moon's views on the probationary year were shared by many of his contemporaries who felt that they were very ill-prepared when they first arrived in India.

His first impressions of India were not encouraging. Travelling northwards into the Punjab he thought it "a terrible dry, unproductive, unattractive country". When he arrived in the Punjab he was "aghast at the flat featureless character of the countryside and the constant wastes of sand and cactus bushes". For administrative purposes, the Punjab was divided into five divisions, each under a Commissioner. The divisions were divided into districts, each under a Deputy Commissioner, or, as the post is often better known, District Officer. The districts were again divided into a number of *tahsils* or administrative units. Moon spent his first 18 months as an Assistant Commissioner stationed at the headquarters of one of the districts. Here, as well as studying for his civil service language and law examinations, he learnt the basics of land revenue administration, essentially the maintenance of village land records which recorded changes in the ownership and tenancy of land and which gave details of the crops grown each harvest in every field. He was also invested as a magistrate with limited powers to try minor cases of assault and theft. There was more than a touch of irony about Moon's training. He was left very much to his own devices and received virtually no guidance from his Deputy Commissioner, an Englishman, who

11 Penderel Moon, in 1940, in full ICS uniform, seated to the right of Sir Henry Craik, Governor of the Punjab.

was in charge of the district as a whole. What little help he received came from an Indian who took over from the English Deputy Commissioner when he went on leave. Having come to India to teach Indians how to govern, Moon had to rely on an Indian to show him how to do it.

In 1934 Moon became District Officer for the district of Multan. The District Officer wore a variety of hats. He was the Collector, responsible for the collection of land revenue and for keeping up-to-date all the land and

12 Moon at his desk when District Officer at Amritsar.

revenue records within his district. He was also the Chief Magistrate, responsible for the work of all the subordinate magistrates within his district and for general control and direction of the police. Finally, as Deputy Commissioner, he was responsible for the general administration of his district.

Multan was one of the largest districts of the Punjab. In 1931 it was just under 6000 square miles in area with a population of just over one million. Moon found his work arduous but never dull. A typical day began at seven in the hot weather (April–September) and ten in the cold (October–March). Time was set aside each day to hear the grievances of petitioners, usually humble peasants complaining either that the *patwari* (the village accountant in charge of village land records) was extracting bribes or, more commonly, "my wife has run away and would the District Officer please try to get her back". Much of the day was spent in court hearing either criminal appeals against lower magistrates' decisions or revenue appeals, involving cases between landlords and tenants. Although it was not common for District Officers to do so, Moon also heard original criminal cases. He now had the power to try all cases punishable by death and to sentence up to seven years. He had regular meetings with district officials of all ranks, including at the higher level the Superintendent of Police, the Public Prosecutor and the Secretary of the District Board. As Chairman of the District Board, Moon presided over meetings which dealt with such matters as public health, primary education and veterinary dispensaries. During the cold weather the District Officer went on tour. Village tours provided an opportunity to look at schools and dispensaries and to check village land records. Moon was surprised to find that urban touring was seldom recommended and yet more often than not it was in the towns that popular discontent with the government existed. He therefore made a point of walking freely through the bazaars of the towns and cities and talking to the craftsmen and shopkeepers.

Increasingly from the 1920s, the maintenance of law and order became a major preoccupation of the District Officer. Multan had a history of communal rioting which frequently occurred during *Muharram*, a Muslim festival commemorating the martyrdom of Husain, grandson of the prophet Muhammad. *Tazias* representing his tomb (usually decorated coffins) were carried in procession. A riot would start when Hindus threw bricks at the *tazias*. Moon recommended immediate and stern action to control such situations:

I was a great believer in the maximum display of force at the very beginning to try and overawe people. I was also a great believer in using force effectively if it had to be used at all. I didn't believe in firing one or two rounds. I used to say to my magistrate, 'If you ever have to open fire, fire at least five rounds, nobody is going to be able to prove that was excessive'. Another thing that we were taught, which is now forgotten, was never to fire over the head of a crowd. If you open fire, make sure that it is effective so that people are seen to fall and the mob takes fright. (*Plain Tales from the Raj*)

Moon did not consider his attitude to be ruthless. On the contrary, he regarded it as "plain common sense".

From Multan, Moon was transferred to the post of District Officer in the district of

13 Moon with Indian servant and garlanded car prior to going on leave from Amritsar.

Gujrat. Then, in 1938, he was appointed Secretary to the Governor of the Punjab. He was now more closely involved with political developments at national level as well as within his own province. When he had first arrived in India in 1929 he had estimated that the British Raj would last for about 25 years, sufficient time in which to fulfil a career and to qualify at the end of it for a pension. He said that had it not been for the Second World War his estimate might well have turned out to be correct. Moon believed that Indian independence was both inevitable and necessary, not only because he considered that Indians were quite capable of governing themselves, but also because he felt that the British could not tackle the main problem of India which was an economic one:

How could the standard of living be raised in this vast land of peasants? I travelled through Russia on my way home on leave in 1937 to see if I could gain any guidance from the USSR. I wanted to give a broadcast talk on it on my return to Lahore but was not allowed to do so. But I felt that a foreign power could not achieve the revolutionary steps that would be necessary to change Indian peasant life. Then I asked myself, 'should one really try to change it?' I can't answer that question. But obviously the Indian intelligentsia wanted to change it and I felt that the British Raj would have to give way to an Indian Raj if any change was to be effected.

Moon became District Officer in Amritsar in 1941 but resigned from the ICS in 1944 and returned to Britain. Two years later he went back to India to become Secretary to a new government Planning Board. In 1947 he was appointed Revenue Minister in the princely state of Bahawalpur, a territory immediately

14 Moon was one of the few ICS men to stay on after independence. Here he greets Jawaharlal Nehru, India's first Prime Minister, at a garden party Simla, 1948.

adjacent to the Punjab. From here he witnessed at first hand the disorders and migrations which accompanied partition. After independence he was one of the few former members of the ICS to remain in service with the new Government of India.

India had not appealed to Moon when he first went there but in time it grew upon him and absorbed his interest. He was aware that the power possessed by a District Officer, which was far more than most individuals were ever likely to exercise, caused a certain amount of arrogance and excessive self-confidence. The mere exercise of power, however, was not, in Moon's case, the principal reward:

As a District Officer you felt that you could, in quite minor ways, help a large number of comparatively helpless people. It was probably an illusion, but this was the satisfaction.

Ed Brown (b. 1904)

Ed Brown enlisted as a "band boy" in the Second Battalion, the Royal Warwickshire

Regiment, in 1918 at the age of 14. He joined the army because, as he later admitted, he had been reading too many adventure stories in comics such as *The Magnet* and *Boy's Own*, which had made him "romantic" in his outlook. His father had been killed during the First World War and he thought he was doing something "romantic" by joining the army "to finish the war off". In 1919 his regiment was posted to India. Brown was excited at the prospect:

My feelings on India before I went there were that it was the glamorous East, beautiful smells, wonderful sight-seeing and altogether a country of mystery. (*Plain Tales from the Raj*)

Many of his companions shared his view that India was a glamorous country. Besides, many of the men in the regiment had no wish to be demobbed at the end of the war. They were tired of the talk of strikes and the lack of food, money and jobs in civilian life. They were, according to Brown, only too pleased to go abroad.

The India that Brown had read about was not the India that he encountered when he arrived. Upon landing at Bombay he was accosted by an Indian woman holding a baby who told him he was the father and asked him for money. Brown and two boys of his own age who were brothers had contracted a fever on the outward voyage. They were detained in hospital for a fortnight and then instructed to catch a train to rejoin their regiment which had been posted to the north-west frontier. Between them, the three boys were given one loaf of bread and a tin of bully-beef for a journey which was supposed to take three days and nights but which actually took five. The brothers fell ill on the journey and they were nearly unconscious when the train eventually reached its destination.

British troops in India had, according to Brown, but one function: "to be on hand in

15 British troops in India.

case of trouble". Keeping the peace amongst the tribesmen of the north-west frontier was a task in itself. Constant vigilance had to be maintained against the Afridis, a Pathan tribe, for whom a British rifle was a much-prized trophy. So adept were they at night-time raids on British camps, that it was not unknown for soldiers to wake in the morning to find that the tents in which they had been sleeping had been stolen. Elsewhere in India, British troops were called upon to deal with disturbances during political demonstrations and communal riots between Hindus and Muslims which often occurred during religious festivals but which increasingly assumed political overtones. On such occasions, Brown sometimes acted as a stretcher-bearer and he remembered one episode which he witnessed when he was stationed at Delhi:

A Muslim had been hanged for committing a murder. His body had been stolen from the jail by his fellow Muslims, his relations and friends. Upon hearing this, the Hindus retaliated. They charged the Muslims, took the body and threw it on to a bullock cart, just like a sack of potatoes. They in turn were charged and the Muslims recovered the body, throwing it back on to their own cart. This went on for perhaps half a day before the troops were called in and the Chief Commissioner was told that he had to act. He told the troops to fix bayonets, which they did, and the natives disappeared. They just went like snow in the sun. The body was eventually recovered and buried in the jail.

Life in general for the ordinary soldier, however, was monotonous and boring. Brown was perhaps fortunate in that he always had his band practices. But for the others, after drill and parade, the day was virtually over by nine o'clock in the morning. Filling, or killing, so much free time was always a problem, particularly in the hot weather when the temperature was often 120° Fahrenheit. As Brown observed, a soldier occupied himself as best he could:

This was mainly done by lying on his bed or playing cards. No other facilities for recreation were available. No encouragement was given to do anything or to learn anything. The soldier sweated it out. Nothing to do from 9 o'clock in the morning until 6 o'clock the next morning. Waiting for the canteen to open or for the *char-wallah*, the tea-server, to come round and taking bets on whether he would be early or late.

16 Pathan tribesmen of India's north-west frontier.

The meals provided for the troops seldom varied and the food was usually infested with flies. The pay was ten shillings a week which rose at the age of 18 to one pound. Out of this, there were certain compulsory purchases: dubbin to clean boots; toothpaste; and polish, with which he rubbed his brass buttons until he could see his face in them. To relieve the boredom, but also to educate himself, Brown spent an additional two rupees a week (about three shillings) on private lessons in Hindustani from a *munshi*.

The social life of the troops was virtually non-existent. Many districts of the large cities were out of bounds because of brothels. Apart from an occasional visit to a local bazaar, the troops were usually confined to barracks. Brown was again more fortunate than most because, as a bandsman, he had the opportunity to perform with the regimental band at official and private engagements.

The only Indians most British soldiers encountered were servants and they seldom came into contact with other Europeans. Brown divided the European community in India into two categories: "The ones in charge and the ones who did the work." He hated the snobbery. On one occasion he was ordered to escort an officer's son back from college. On the train he occupied the same compartment as an officer and two high-ranking British women who never spoke to him for the entire journey.

Although Brown took pride in his performance and was grateful that the army had given him the opportunity to learn music, he was glad when he left India in 1929. But what he remembered most were the great contrasts of India: fabulous wealth on the one hand; disease, poverty and hunger on the other. He was critical of the British role in India:

India was a waste from the ordinary soldier's point of view and looking back on it I think the British Government missed an opportunity. They could have made India a vast country of agriculture and industry. The population looked upon British royalty as Gods and Goddesses. Nothing was done to stem the tide of disease, misery and poverty. This is talking as a soldier. I don't know how the civilians looked at it but I think they looked on Indians as just cattle, people who made up a number.

By now 25, Brown recalled the return voyage and his first glimpse of the English coast a day out of Southampton. It was "the most beautiful sight I've ever seen in my life". When he landed at Southampton it was snowing. The troops had to make their own way back to the regiment's barracks in the Midlands.

THE INDIAN NATIONALISTS

This section, which is based on the careers of three of the most prominent nationalist politicians, examines the following key issues: the nature of Gandhi's appeal as leader of the nationalist movement, the effectiveness of non-violence as a political weapon, and the reasons why, in 1947, India was partitioned.

The turning point for the nationalist movement in India occurred at the end of the First World War. Before this time, with the exception of a brief period of revolutionary agitation which followed Lord Curzon's partition of Bengal in 1905, Indian nationalism had been led by moderates who were not prepared to go outside the law in expressing their dissatisfaction with British rule. At the end of the war, these same nationalists expected major changes in British policy. In 1917, in recognition of the valuable contribution made by India to the war effort, the government in London issued a statement defining the goal of British policy in India as "the progressive realisation of responsible government". But the subsequent Government of India Act of 1919, providing for Indians to exercise a limited degree of control over their own affairs in the provinces of British India, fell well short of nationalist expectations. The Amritsar Massacre of 1919 added further fuel to nationalist resentment. General Dyer, a British officer in the Indian army, exacted a fearful revenge for riots in Amritsar which had claimed the lives of four Europeans. Without warning, he ordered his men to open fire at a public meeting attended by several thousand unarmed Indians. Official figures put the casualties at 379 dead and over

18 The first Indian National Congress, 1885. The early Congress was a middle-class political movement consisting of professional men such as lawyers and journalists. Not until the 1920s did it become a popular movement.

1200 wounded. Gandhi, until now a loyal subject of the British empire, wrote in *Young India*, the newspaper of which he was editor:

To my amazement and dismay, I have discovered that the present representatives of the Empire . . . have no real regard for the wishes of the people of India and they count Indian honour as of little consequence. I can no longer retain affection for a government so evilly manned as it is nowadays.

Preaching non-violence, Gandhi led the Indian National Congress through three political campaigns against the British: non-cooperation in 1920, civil disobedience in 1930, and Quit India in 1942. In the process, Congress was transformed. It ceased to be an élite, middle-class organization dominated by lawyers. It become a mass popular movement, with committees and officials in every province and with a membership reaching down to the villages. As the Congress juggernaut gathered momentum, so tensions developed within its ranks. Gandhi's leadership was not always accepted without question. Gandhi fought a running battle with the Congress radicals who were never entirely happy with non-violence and who pressed for the adoption of socialist policies. But Subhas Chandra Bose, one of Gandhi's main critics, acknowledged that Gandhi had a unique appeal for India's masses:

His simple life, his vegetarian diet, his goat's milk, his day of silence every week, his habit of squatting on the floor instead of sitting on a chair, his loincloth − in fact everything connected with him − has marked him out as one of the eccentric Mahatmas of old and has brought him nearer to his people. . . . When he talks to them about Swaraj, he does not dilate on the virtues of provincial autonomy or federation, he reminds them of the glories of *Ramarajya* [the kingdom of King Rama of old] and they understand.

Bose wondered, however, what would have happened to Gandhi in a different environment:

WHEN EAST MEETS EAST
"Come in and take a seat."
[Mr. Gandhi and Mr. Jinnah are expected to meet this month.]

19 Political deadlock. The Gandhi-Jinnah talks on the Muslim demand for Pakistan, which were held in September 1944, ended in failure.

Born in another country he might have been a complete misfit. What, for instance, would he have done in a country like Russia or Germany or Italy? His doctrine of non-violence would have led him to the cross or to the mental hospital.

Throughout its history, Congress had claimed to represent all Indians, irrespective of their caste or religion. This claim was ultimately rejected by the leaders of India's Muslims. As a minority community, albeit a substantial one (Muslims formed one-fifth of India's total population), the Muslims feared that they would be at a permanent disadvantage under a representative system based on a mere counting of heads. Always anxious to blunt the edge of the Congress appeal, the British were more than willing to introduce safeguards for the Muslims. In 1906, an All-India Muslim League was established. Three years later a separate Muslim electorate was introduced. In future Muslim voters would elect Muslim candidates to fill a number of seats reserved for Muslims on the legislative councils. By this means the Muslims obtained greater parliamentary representation than their numbers alone would justify. Congress attacked what it regarded as "divide and rule" tactics but the Muslims did not regard themselves as tools of British imperialism. Their dilemma, they believed, was real enough. As Muhammad Ali (not to be confused with Mahomed Ali Jinnah, the leader of the Muslims League) put it in 1930:

Where God commands . . . I am a Muslim first, a Muslim second and a Muslim last and nothing but a Muslim. . . . But where India is concerned, where India's freedom is concerned, I am an Indian first, an Indian second, an Indian last and nothing but an Indian. . . . I belong to two circles of equal size . . . India and the Muslim world . . . and can leave neither.

The British created the conditions which made it possible for the Muslims to claim separate statehood. Congress committed tactical errors in its dealings with the Muslim League and under-estimated the appeal of religion in politics. Islamic theorists argued the case for Pakistan. All three explain why, by 1947, the Indian Muslims had abandoned any attempt to reconcile the two worlds to which they belonged.

Jawaharlal Nehru (1889-1964)

Jawaharlal Nehru was born in 1889, the son of a successful and wealthy Brahmin lawyer. As a boy, and indeed as a young man, Nehru was spoilt by his doting father who was determined that his son should have the best English education that money could buy. From 1905, Nehru spent seven years in England, first at Harrow, then at Cambridge University and finally at the Inner Temple in London where he qualified as a barrister. In London, he lived the life of an aristocratic Edwardian gentleman. His annual expenses, provided by his father, rose above £800, enough then to support a comfortable existence in the capital for three years. Nehru's lifestyle contrasted with that of Gandhi who, as a young law student in London during the 1880s, spent only six pence a day on three meals.

When he returned to India in 1912 it was not law that interested Nehru but politics, a

20   A family group taken in 1909 when Nehru was 20.

subject in which he had shown a passionate interest from an early age. He had been thrilled by the news of Japan's victory over Russia in the Far East in 1905, the first time in modern history that an Asian nation had defeated a European power. Japan's victory gave Nehru the confidence to believe that the whole of Asia, including India, could one day rid itself of Western colonialism. India's problem, however, was one of finding the means with which to mount an effective challenge to British rule. Neither of the alternatives which had been tried in the past seemed appropriate to Nehru. He regarded terrorist extremism as self-defeating because it only invited further repression, while constitutional politics, with the emphasis on long speeches and wordy resolutions, was equally unacceptable because it seemed to leave the British free to decide whether or not to grant reforms as if they were handing out rewards for good behaviour.

Gandhi's *satyagraha* (force born of non-violence) suggested a new way forward.

21 Nehru with Gandhi at a Congress meeting in Bombay in 1942. Note the Congress flag, which became India's national flag, in the background.

Nehru was immediately impressed by the possibilities. He recalled in his *Autobiography: Towards Freedom:*

When I first read about this proposal in the newspapers my first reaction was one of tremendous relief. Here at last was a way out of the tangle, a method of action which was straight and open and possibly effective.

Gandhi and Nehru were like father and son but they did not always see eye-to-eye. Indeed, in many respects they were poles apart in their political outlook. Gandhi condemned what he regarded as the evils of modern industrial society and idealized instead village India which represented traditional Hindu virtues such as respect for life and the individual and the absence of competition. A convert to socialism during his European travels in the 1920s, Nehru disagreed. It was not Western influences as such that Nehru resented; merely the fact that one Western power was denying freedom to India. For all their differences, however, Nehru and Gandhi were always close because the one recognized in the other attributes which were essential to the nationalist

struggle. For Gandhi, Nehru was a means both to broaden the appeal of Congress, because of his following amongst the young, and to maintain Congress unity, because he enjoyed the support of the Congress radicals. On four occasions – 1929-30, 1936, 1937 and 1940 – Nehru was chosen as Congress President. On each occasion, Gandhi's backing was decisive. For Nehru, Gandhi was indispensable to the nationalist movement. His secret dread was that Gandhi would die during one of his many fasts. Gandhi's unique ability to reach out to the masses and to inspire them was, in Nehru's eyes, adequate compensation for Gandhi's many inconsistencies and eccentricities. Nehru wrote of the salt march in his autobiography:

As we saw the abounding enthusiasm of the people and the way salt-making was spreading like a prairie fire, we felt a little ashamed for having questioned the efficacy of this method when it was first proposed by Gandhiji. And we marvelled at the amazing knack of the man to impress the multitude and make it act in an organised way.

Until 1947, Nehru dedicated his life to the nationalist struggle. He spent nine years in nine different jails between 1921 and 1945. He abandoned the lifestyle of his youth and took to wearing home-spun *khadi* clothes. He travelled extensively throughout India and drew large crowds wherever he spoke. He listened sympathetically to the grievances of the peasants for whom the very name of Nehru always meant more than what he actually said to them.

But in one vital respect Nehru, and indeed the entire Congress movement, had to admit failure. The dream that India would become free but remain united was shattered in 1947 when independence was accompanied by partition. Many historians believe that Congress policies actually stimulated the Muslim demand for a separate Muslim state. At a time when his own international outlook led him to envisage the future in terms of world organizations and large multi-national states, Nehru could not but regard the

22   Nehru in 1946 when the Cabinet Mission visited India.

Pakistan movement as being out of step with the logic of history. He regarded the leaders of the Muslim League as narrow-minded reactionaries who whipped up the religious fanaticism of their own community merely to gain power for themselves. Indeed on one occasion he likened the outlook of the Muslim League to that prevailing in the Middle Ages. The emphasis which the League placed on the differences between Hindus and Muslims did little more in Nehru's eyes than provide the British with a ready-made excuse to justify the continuation of their own rule in India.

In order to prove that Congress was the only genuine "nationalist" party, Nehru, in the late 1930s, attempted to uproot the Muslim League. Congress won a handsome majority in the election of 1937 in the United Provinces, Nehru's home province. The Muslim League asked for the formation of a coalition government including Muslims who were members of the League. Nehru replied that any Muslims chosen would first have to give up their League affiliation and join

Congress. He expected that other provinces would follow suit, but the Muslim League refused to accept these terms. The events in a single province of British India in 1937 did not, of course, make partition inevitable; it was not until 1940 that the Muslim League put forward its "Pakistan" demand and even then there was still a long way to go. Nonetheless, the attitude of Nehru and Congress certainly had the opposite effect to that intended. Under the leadership of Mahomed Ali Jinnah, the attitude of the Muslim League hardened. Jinnah was determined that the Leage should not go into voluntary liquidation. He set himself the task of strengthening it in order that Congress should recognize it as an equal. With support from the Muslim masses, he was determined to prove that the League alone, not Congress, represented the interests of India's Muslim population. Upon this basis, the demand for Pakistan was built. By 1947, by which time the demand had become irresistible, Nehru and Congress had only two options: to concede or to face the prospect of civil war. For Nehru in particular the prospect of civil war was unthinkable and so, with reluctance, he accepted partition. Unintentionally, Nehru and Congress had contributed to what they had always been most anxious to avoid.

Between 1947 and his death in 1964, Nehru governed as India's first Prime Minister. He launched the "green" revolution, which was designed to increase agricultural output through the introduction of improved seeds and the construction of irrigation works, and also a series of five-year plans in which the main emphasis was on the expansion of India's industrial base. Abroad, he championed the interests of the Third World and became one of the founders of the non-aligned movement which aimed to reduce international tensions by encouraging as many countries as possible to steer clear of the rival power blocs led by the United States and the Soviet Union.

Nehru was not without his faults. There was a streak of vanity in his character and he was always susceptible to flattery. More a man of ideas than an organizer or manager, he possessed neither the ruthlessness nor perhaps the ability to stamp out the infighting and corruption which had become features of Congress politics. Nevertheless, adored by the people of his own country and respected by the international community at large, he is still remembered as one of the most popular leaders of the twentieth century.

Mahomed Ali Jinnah (1876-1948)

Born in Karachi in 1876, the eldest of seven children of a hide merchant, Mahomed Ali Jinnah commenced his legal studies at Lincoln's Inn in London at the age of 16 and became, two years later, the youngest Indian student ever to be called to the Bar. He returned to India in 1896. Jinnah progressed in life the hard way. He lost his mother while he was still in London and, during his early twenties, he became responsible for supporting his family after the failure of his father's business. By virtue of hard work, assisted by some shrewd investments on the stock market, he amassed a personal fortune. By 1940, he had no less than four large residential properties in New Delhi and Bombay, the city in which he had established his legal practice.

Tall, thin and drawn, immaculately dressed in Saville Row suits and sporting a monocle, Jinnah was always a controversial figure. The British, who frequently regarded him as an awkward customer, maintained that he was aloof and haughty, inflexible and uncompromising. More than one British observer commented on how Jinnah seemed to lack the warmth of a Gandhi or a Nehru and how he had no time for small talk or trivialities. Lord Mountbatten, the last Viceroy, despaired of Jinnah. Mountbatten thought the idea of Pakistan "sheer madness" and he wrote:

I regard Jinnah as a psychopathic case; in fact until I met him I would not have thought it possible that a man with such a complete lack of administrative knowledge or sense of responsibility could achieve or hold down so powerful a position. (*The Transfer of Power in India*, 1942-7)

Some of the Congress leaders went even further in their criticisms. They had long believed that Jinnah was motivated by personal ambition, pride and vanity but in the final phases before partition some of them ascribed more sinister motives to him. Vallabhbhai Patel, a senior Congressman, believed that Jinnah wanted to establish "a form of Fascist dictatorship with ultimate designs against the Government of India".

It is perhaps not surprising that Pakistani scholars and observers have since leapt to Jinnah's defence. Many have commented on how Jinnah's personality was transformed as a result of his separation from his second wife in

24 Jinnah as a young law student in London.

25 A rare moment of harmony: Jinnah (right) takes a stroll with Nehru, May 1946.

1928 and her death the following year. Once a cheerful and sociable individual, he became lonely and withdrawn. Nevertheless, Jinnah is still seen as a considerate and caring human being. He took great care to provide for the well-being of his servants, replied personally to nearly every letter he received, and insisted on signing himself every Muslim Leaguer's subscription receipt as a means of cementing the ties that bound him to his supporters. In the words of Z.H. Zaidi, a Pakistani historian:

How could the autocratic, cold, calculating figure of popular myth have attracted the loyalty and affection of so many prominent and experienced politicians, and of countless party workers? It was not as a dictator that he exercised power, but as a man able to charm friends and enemies alike into compliance. ("M.A. Jinnah: The Man" from *World Scholars on Quaid-i-Azam*)

Whatever the difference of opinion about his character, there can be little doubt, at least at the beginning of his career, that Jinnah was a staunch Indian nationalist. He was a member of Congress before the Muslim League was formed and acted as secretary to the Congress President at the first session of Congress he attended in 1906. When he joined the League in 1913, he maintained that his support for Muslim interests could not override his loyalty to the wider nationalist cause. Early in his career he was also a champion of Hindu-Muslim unity and it was largely owing to his efforts that, at the time of the First World War, the League agreed to hold its annual sessions at the same time and in the same place as Congress. When League and Congress assembled at Lucknow in 1916, a pact was negotiated whereby Congress, reversing its former position, agreed that Muslims should continue to be elected by separate electorates and that they should have more seats in the central and provincial legislatures than their numbers alone would justify. Jinnah viewed separate electorates at this time as a temporary measure which was necessary to reassure the Muslims:

A minority must, above everything else, have a complete sense of security before its broader political sense can be evoked for co-operation and united endeavour in the national task. To the Musalmans of India that security can only come through effective safeguards as regards their political existence as a community.

In 1920, however, Jinnah parted company from Congress. He was out of place when, under the impact of Gandhi's leadership, Congress ceased to be an élite, middle-class organization consisting mainly of lawyers like himself and became instead a mass, popular movement. Jinnah opposed Gandhi's non-cooperation movement, arguing, as a strictly constitutional politician, that opposition should be conducted within the confines of the law. He moved still further away from Congress in 1928 when an All-Parties Convention approved the report of the Motilal Nehru Committee which not only demanded Dominion Status but also recommended the abolition of separate electorates. Jinnah remarked sadly to a friend, "this is the parting of the ways". He became disillusioned and although he attended two of the Round Table conferences in London in 1930 and 1931, he effectively retired from politics. He remained in London with his daughter and sister and concentrated on his legal career.

Persuaded by some prominent Muslims that his leadership was needed, Jinnah returned to India in 1934 and became President of the Muslim League. The provincial elections of 1937 gave Jinnah the impetus he needed. The results were a setback for the League: of the total 482 seats allotted to the Muslims, it won only 109 and it made little impression in the four Muslim-majority provinces of Bengal, the Punjab, Sind and the North-West Frontier Province. But it was the terms insisted upon by Congress for the formation of coalition governments in the Hindu-majority provinces – essentially that the League should disband itself – that really angered Jinnah. To force Congress to recognize the League as an equal, Jinnah reformed the League and extended its membership from a few thousand in 1937 to several hundred thousand by the outbreak of the Second World War. Jinnah also set out to convince the ordinary Muslim that Muslim interests would be in grave danger if Congress alone came to power when the British eventually withdrew. Congress India, he said, would be a Hindu India. Given that Congress symbolism – its flag, its national anthem, its language policy – were all derived from Hindu influences, the arguments of Jinnah and the League began to sound persuasive for the ordinary Muslim. In the autumn of 1939, when the Congress governments in the provinces resigned because they had not been consulted before the government announced that India was also at war with Germany, Jinnah called upon Muslims everywhere to observe "Deliverance Day".

Jinnah did not create the Pakistan demand. The idea of a separate Muslim state based on the Muslim majority areas of the north-west of India had been first suggested in 1930 by Dr Muhammad Iqbal, a poet-philosopher from the Punjab. The idea was developed in the late Thirties by several prominent Muslims and extended to include the Muslim majority areas of the north-east. When it met at Lahore in March 1940, the Muslim League called officially for the creation of independent Muslim "states" in the north-western and north-eastern zones of India. Jinnah had now formed the opinion that Western-style democracy was unsuitable for India and in his speech at Lahore he declared that India represented not one, but two quite distinct and separate nations:

The Hindus and Muslims belong to two different religious philosophies, social customs and literature. They neither intermarry, nor interdine together and indeed they belong to two different civilisations which are based mainly on conflicting ideas and conceptions. . . . To yoke together two such nations under a single state, one as a numerical minority and the other as a majority, must lead to growing discontent and the final destruction of any fabric that may be so built up for the government of such a state.

During the war, Jinnah never argued that he would accept nothing less than Pakistan. He did, however, insist that the Muslim League would not accept any political settlement that would make the attainment of Pakistan impossible. In other words, he wanted to keep his options open. To safeguard Muslim interests, he insisted that the Muslims should have an absolute veto over any constitutional scheme to which they were opposed and that the Muslim League should have parity with Congress in any central government that might be established. The pace quickened at the end of the war when the Labour government elected in Britain in 1945 pledged itself to an early and complete withdrawal from India. A Cabinet Mission which was sent to India in the spring of 1946 suggested, as a means to keep India united, a federation based

TODAY IS———

DIRECT ACTION DAY

TODAY MUSLIMS OF INDIA DEDICATE ANEW THEIR LIVES AND ALL THEY POSSESS TO THE CAUSE OF FREEDOM

TODAY LET EVERY MUSLIM SWEAR IN THE NAME OF ALLAH TO RESIST AGGRESSION

DIRECT ACTION IS NOW THEIR ONLY COURSE

BECAUSE———

★ They offered Peace but Peace was spurned
★ They honoured their word but were betrayed
★ They claimed Liberty but are offered Thraldom

NOW MIGHT ALONE CAN SECURE THEIR RIGHT

PLEDGE OF SACRIFICE

At The Convention Of National Legislators Held In Delhi On April 9-10, 1946, They Took The Following Pledge

In the name of Allah, the Beneficent the Merciful.

"Say: my prayer and my sacrifice and my living and my dying are all for Allah, the Lord of the Worlds" (Al Quran).

I M. A. Jinnah, a member of the Muslim League Party of the Central Legislative Assembly do hereby solemnly declare my firm conviction that the safety and security, and the salvation and destiny of the Muslim nation inhabiting the sub-continent of India lie only in the achievement of Pakistan which is the one equitable, honourable and just solution of the constitutional problem and which will bring peace, freedom and prosperity to the various nationalities and communities of this great sub-continent.

I most solemnly affirm that I shall willingly and unflinchingly carry out all the directions and instructions which may be issued by the All-India Muslim League in pursuance of any movement launched by it for the attainment of the cherished national goal of Pakistan, and, believing as I do in the rightness and the justice of my cause, I pledge myself to undergo any danger, trial or sacrifice which may be demanded of me.

"Our Lord! Bestow on us endurance, and keep our steps firm and help us against the disbelieving people." Amen!

Signature........M.A.Jinnah

Dated....9th April 1946........

TODAY LET EVERY MUSLIM ALSO TAKE THIS PLEDGE OF SACRIFICE THE CAUSE OF NATIONAL FREEDOM

PAKISTAN IS OURS

★ BY RIGHT OF NATIONHOOD ★
★ BY RIGHT OF MAJORITY ★
★ BY RIGHT OF NATIONAL JUSTICE ★
★ BY RIGHT OF POPULAR VERDICT ★

WE SHALL FIGHT FOR IT . . . . . .
. . . . WE SHALL DIE FOR IT
TAKE IT WE MUST—OR PERISH

THE RESOLUTION

THE FOLLOWING IS THE FULL TEXT OF THE DIRECT ACTION RESOLUTION PASSED UNANIMOUSLY BY THE MUSLIM NATIONAL PARLIAMENT, BOMBAY, ON JULY 29, 1946:

"Whereas the All-India Muslim League has today to reject the proposals embodied in the statement of Cabinet Delegation and the Viceroy dated May 16, 1946, due intransigence of the Congress on the one hand and the breach of faith with the Muslims by the British Government on the other;

"And whereas Muslim India has exhausted without all efforts to find a peaceful solution of the Indian problem by compromise and constitutional means; and whereas the Congress is bent upon setting up a caste-Hindu Raj in India with the connivance of the British; and whereas recent events have shown that power politics and not justice and fairplay are deciding factors in Indian affairs;

Achievement Of Pakistan

"And whereas it has become abundantly clear that the Muslims of India would not rest content with anything less than the immediate establishment of an Independent and full Sovereign Pakistan and would resist any attempt to impose any constitution, long-term or short-term, or the setting up of any Interim Government at the Centre without the approval and consent of the Muslims, the Council of the All-India Muslim League is convinced that now the time has come for the Muslim Nation to resort to Direct Action to achieve Pakistan and to get rid of the present slavery under the British and contemplated future caste-Hindu domination."

Be Ready For Every Sacrifice

"This Council calls upon the Muslim Nation to stand to a man behind their sole representative organisation—the All-India Muslim League—and be ready for every sacrifice.

"This Council directs the Working Committee to prepare forthwith a programme of Direct Action to carry out the policy initiated above and to organise the Muslims for the coming struggle to be launched as and when necessary.

"As a protest against and in token of their deep resentment of the attitude of the British, this Council calls upon the Musalmans to renounce forthwith the titles conferred upon them by the Alien Government."

IT IS NOW FOR THE NATION TO CARRY IT O

26-29 *Dawn* was launched by Jinnah in October 1941 as a weekly English-language newspaper to express Mulsim opinion. The issue for 16 August 1946 proclaims the Muslim League's "Direct Action Day".

on three regional groups of provinces. The Mission also proposed names for an interim government which would function until a new Indian constitution had been drawn up. Congress and the League, however, placed different interpretations on the Mission's proposals and no agreement was possible. Amidst bitter recriminations on both sides, Jinnah called, in August 1946, for a Muslim "Day of Action" which produced over 4000 deaths in Calcutta alone.

By the time the government in London announced in February 1947 that power would be transferred to Indian hands by a date not later than June 1948 (it was Lord Mountbatten who brought the date forward to August 1947), Jinnah was adamant in his demand for partition. Instead of the independent Muslim "states" suggested in 1940, the demand now was for the single state of Pakistan, the two halves of which would be

separated by over a thousand miles of Indian territory. But just as Congress failed to achieve a united India, so Jinnah failed to achieve the Pakistan that he wanted. The partition argument was turned against him. If India had to be divided, so too did the provinces that would be affected. Jinnah wanted Pakistan to include the whole of Bengal and the Punjab. Congress, however, insisted that the Hindu areas of West Bengal and East Punjab should remain with India. Mountbatten hoped that the prospect of a "moth-eaten" Pakistan might make Jinnah think twice. It did not. A Boundary Commission was appointed to determine the lines of partition in Bengal and the Punjab. In the final hectic weeks of British rule, Jinnah's life was threatened by the more extreme Sikh leaders whose homeland was destined to be cut in two by the partition of the Punjab. Mountbatten accompanied Jinnah

30 Jinnah with Lord Mountbatten at Karachi after Jinnah had been sworn in as the first Governor-General of Pakistan, 14 August 1947. They are followed by Jinnah's sister and Lady Mountbatten.

during the independence celebrations in Karachi on 14 August 1947 and described the scene in the last report he wrote as Viceroy:

The State procession took place in open cars, with Jinnah and myself in the leading car and my wife and Miss Jinnah in the next car. The route was fairly thickly lined with enthusiastic crowds, which were kept back by troops and police lining the route. As we turned in at the gates of Government House, Jinnah put his hand on my knee and said with deep emotion, 'Thank God I have brought you back alive'! I retorted by pointing out how much more serious it would have been if he had been bumped off. (*The Transfer of Power in India, 1942-7*)

Upon independence, Jinnah became Pakistan's first Governor-General. He died soon after of a heart attack in February 1948. He suffered from tuberculosis and had, in fact, been ill for some time. His illness had been kept a closely guarded secret; not even Mountbatten knew about it. Many have since pondered what might have happened had he died earlier or had the British held on a little longer. In an age sceptical of the role of "great men" in history, there are still those who believe that Jinnah alone brought Pakistan into being. Whatever the truth, he is revered to this day in Pakistan as *Quaid-i-Azam* – The Great Leader.

Subhas Chandra Bose (1897-1945)

In the early hours of 17 January 1941, disguised in a long coat and a black fez as Mohammed Ziauddin, a travelling inspector with an insurance company, Subhas Chandra Bose slipped secretly out of his home in Calcutta in Bengal. Bose had been arrested by the British, for the eleventh time, in July 1940. In prison he had gone on hunger strike causing his health to deteriorate to such an extent that he was released and allowed home but kept under police surveillance. He was due to appear in court on 27 January 1941 on a charge of sedition. Bose's arrest in the summer of 1940 had coincided with the fall of France to Germany and he seems then to have made up his mind that the time had come for him to go abroad. Convinced that Britain would eventually lose the war, Bose believed that the presence of a representative of a new nationalist government of India would be needed at a post-war peace conference to ensure that India obtained the full

31 Subhas Chandra Bose.

independence to which she had long aspired. He was, therefore, anxious to make contact with such powers as would help in the liberation of India from British rule.

Assisted by his cousin and a small group of trusted friends, Bose travelled from his home by car to a small wayside station in the Bihar countryside some 200 miles from Calcutta. From here he boarded the night train to Delhi and then the frontier mail to Peshawar on the north-west frontier. A further journey, first by car and then on foot, took him through the rugged terrain of the Khyber pass and on to Kabul, the capital of Afghanistan. After five frustrating days, attempting unsuccessfully to make contact with the Russian embassy, he was greatly relieved to accept an offer of assistance from the Italian legation. With a passport in the name of Orlando Massotta, he made a further hazardous journey to the Russian frontier and took a train to Moscow from where, on 28 March 1941, he flew to Berlin.

Bose's "escape" from India in 1941 was the latest in a long line of extraordinary episodes which had occurred at regular intervals throughout his career. Born at Cuttack in Orissa in 1897, he was educated in Calcutta and made Bengal his political base. Suspected of having instigated an assault on an English history professor whose racial insults had infuriated the students, he was expelled from his college in 1916. In 1919 he reluctantly bowed to his father's wishes and travelled to England to prepare for the ICS exam. "What gives me the greatest joy", he wrote to a friend from Cambridge, "is to watch the whiteskins serving me and cleaning my shoes". He passed the exam in 1920 but resigned soon after and returned to India to offer his services during the non-cooperation movement. As a leading organizer of the attempt to boycott a visit by the Prince of Wales to Calcutta, he was arrested in 1921 and sentenced to six months' imprisonment. Expecting a much longer sentence, he turned to the magistrate and said: "Only six months. Have I then stolen a chicken?" Upon his release he became Mayor of Calcutta. Suspected of supporting terrorists, he was arrested again in 1924, never

formally charged, and transferred in 1925 to the prison fortress of Mandalay in Burma where he spent the next two years. He was arrested on three separate occasions during the civil disobedience movement and exiled from India in 1933. Although barred from entering Britain, he travelled extensively in Europe and spent much of his time writing *The Indian Struggle*, a personal account of the nationalist movement. The book criticized Gandhi, in particular, for suspending civil disobedience and negotiating a peace formula with Irwin, and called for a change in both the leadership and methods of Congress. It also revealed the extent to which Bose's own political thinking had been influenced by both Communism and Fascism. He urged the formation of a new political party and gave a brief outline of how it should be organized and what its ideology should be:

The party will stand for the interests of the masses . . . . It will believe in a sound system of state planning for the reorganisation of the agricultural and industrial life of the country. . . . It will not stand for democracy in the Mid-Victorian sense of the term, but will believe in government by a strong party bound together by military discipline.

Although by now at odds with the mainstream of the nationalist movement, Bose returned to India in 1936 as a great celebrity and with a reputation rivalling that of Gandhi and Nehru. He was elected Congress President in 1938 and 1939, the second time against Gandhi's wishes. Forced by Gandhi to resign in April 1939, Bose urged Congress to launch a national revolution to overthrow British rule when war broke out in September. His speeches to this effect, which led to his arrest in 1940, failed to move the Congress leadership. It was at this point that Bose decided to seek foreign support in the liberation of India.

Following his escape from India, Bose spent two years in Berlin. He was under no illusions about his hosts but turned a blind eye to the excesses of the Nazi régime: "My enemy's enemy is my friend" became his motto. Still

32 "A dangerous revolutionary": a government of India telegram about Bose.

using his Italian name he spent much of his time preparing and then broadcasting anti-British propaganda. But this was a particularly frustrating period for Bose. The Germans refused to adopt the liberation of India as one of their war aims and he was thus unable to persuade them to establish a Free India government in Europe. At his one and only meeting with Hitler in May 1942 Bose was shown a wall map indicating the location of the German divisions in Russia and the distance which separated them from India. Hitler saw fit to remind Bose that "the power of a country could only be exercised within the range of its sword".

Japan's entry into the war in December 1941 and the British surrender at Singapore in February 1942 opened up new possibilities for Bose. With the British in retreat in the Far East it was obvious that Japan could do much more to assist Bose than Germany. Leaving Germany by U-boat in February 1943, Bose was transferred in April to a Japanese submarine off the coast of Mozambique in East Africa. He arrived in Tokyo in May.

After talks with General Tojo, Japan's Prime Minister, he was on the move again, this time to Singapore where he received a rapturous welcome from the Indian community and assumed the leadership of the Indian independence movement in East Asia.

Convinced now that he was on the threshold of a great victory, Bose began to display signs of megalomania. Known as *Netaji*, the Indian equivalent of Führer or Leader, he discarded his civilian clothes for an imposing military uniform and demanded the rights and privileges of a head of state. On his travels to the Japanese-occupied territories of Burma, Malaya and Thailand he was accompanied by Japanese military jeeps mounted with machine-guns, a cavalcade of cars and motor-cycle outriders. At Singapore in October 1943 he established a Provisional Government of India which consisted of four ministers. Bose himself became Head of State, Prime Minister, Minister of War and Foreign Minister.

To lead an Indian army in the liberation of his country was now Bose's greatest ambition. At Singapore he inherited the remnants of the Indian National Army (INA) which the Japanese had formed in 1942 from deserters and prisoners-of-war. This first INA had more or less disintegrated under the impact of Japanese arrogance, Indian mistrust of Japanese intentions and divisions amongst the

33 Bose (garlanded centre) at a political meeting in Bengal, 1938.

Indians themselves. Bose wanted to rebuild it into a force for the invasion of India. An INA of three million men became his target. The Japanese never took him seriously; they could only afford to equip 30,000.

Units of the INA, about 8000 men, saw action during the Imphal campaign in 1944. Imphal was the capital of Manipur, a territory in the far north-east of India adjacent to the Burmese frontier. If it could be captured, so Bose believed, it would be of enormous psychological value. It would be the first time that the British had been defeated on Indian soil and it would encourage the outbreak of revolution in India. The campaign, however, turned out to be a disaster. The INA and the Japanese troops with whom they fought were outnumbered by the British forces commanded by General Slim who had the advantage of air superiority. The Japanese and the INA were forced to retreat in July 1944. Inadequate rations and medical supplies destroyed the morale of the men in the INA. Discipline began to disintegrate and desertions became commonplace.

For Bose, Imphal was the beginning of the end. Totally dependent on Japanese support, he became a helpless bystander as Japan's intended Asian empire, the Co-Prosperity Sphere, began to collapse. On 15 August 1945 Japan surrendered. Three days later, attempting to make contact with the Russians in Manchuria, Bose was killed in a plane crash.

Today in India Bose is a national hero. Buildings, roads, parks and lakes are named after him and his statue stands in city squares where once stood statues of British Kings and Queens and Viceroys. His daring, his reckless courage and his spirit of self-sacrifice captured the imagination of India. For all his undeniable faults, he proved that Indians were prepared to fight, and to die, for the cause of their country's freedom. The British themselves contributed to his martyrdom. At the end of the war key members of the INA were put on trial in the Red Fort in Delhi.

34 Propaganda poster used by Indian National Army agents on the Burma front during the Second World War.

Accused of waging war against the King-Emperor, they were found guilty and sentenced to transportation for life. As news of the exploits of the INA began to filter through to the Indian public, a national outcry ensued. Nehru, who appeared in court as a defence counsel, summed up the mood when he remarked that the trial had dramatized the old contest – England versus India – and that it had in effect become "a trial of strength between the will of the Indian people and the will of those who hold power in India". Persuaded of the strength of public feeling by strikes and by a mutiny in the Royal Indian Navy, the British were forced to abandon any further INA trials. At the height of the controversy questions were asked about the circumstances of Bose's death. Many, including Gandhi, referred to him as if he were still alive. Since independence in 1947 the evidence has been examined by two commissions of enquiry appointed by the Government of India. Both concluded that Bose died in a plane crash in 1945 but there are still those who refuse to accept this. In January of each year many Indians celebrate the anniversary of Bose's birth as if he were still alive. One day, it is said, he will return.

THE BRITISH COMMUNITY IN INDIA

British officials, whether civilian or military, represented only a small fraction of the total British community that lived and worked in India. As well as the memsahibs and their children, there were businessmen and tea-planters, doctors and nurses, engineers and surveyors, missionaries and governesses, journalists and teachers. Many went out in their twenties to pursue careers or, in the case of some of the women, to find husbands. But, for others, India was much more than a place to live and work: it was, until independence in 1947, the only home they had ever known. Some were born in India; others were born in Britain and taken to India when they were very young. Many were the third or fourth generations of families who could trace their connections with India back to the time of the East India Company in the eighteenth century.

This section examines the experiences in India of three members of the British community: a memsahib, a tea-planter and a missionary. It looks in particular at their lifestyles and living conditions and also at their attitudes towards Indians and the independence movement.

The twentieth-century British community in India lived a strange sort of twilight existence. Clothes and some customs had changed but social standards and the lifestyle in general were still firmly rooted in the late Victorian and early Edwardian eras. Socially conservative and tradition-bound, the British were punctilious in everything they did. They had to contend with the extremes of the Indian climate and many lived in remote up-country areas where there was no electricity, tap-water or air-conditioning. Whatever their circumstances, however, they never allowed their standards to drop. Even young bachelors living alone on isolated tea-gardens

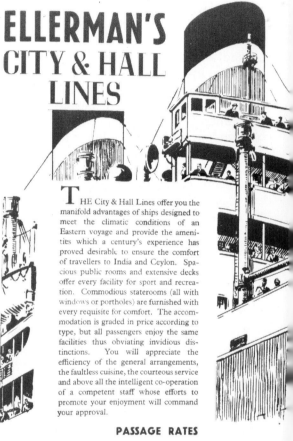

35 A passage to India: the cheapest rates in 1939.

(plantations) in the middle of the Assam forest made a point of dressing for dinner. Always conscious that they were so few ruling so many, the British were obsessed with keeping up appearances.

street or when out riding, it was always the Indian who had to make way for the Briton. Attitudes began to change after the First World War but only slowly. Francis Smyth, the wife of an army officer in India in the 1920s, likened the change of attitude to the emancipation of women in Britain:

In my day in India it was rather like that. We were just beginning to accept Indians as equals – just.

A number of British civilians were critical of British rule in India but the majority were proud of what they considered to have been major British achievements: the British had

36 The memsahib in India: a District Officer's wife in 1916.

Apart from their work, the only contact that most of the British, certainly the women, had with Indians was through their servants. Every bachelor had a valet or bearer and every household with very young children had an *ayah*, an Indian nanny or nurse. Although the British were sometimes entertained by the Indian aristocracy, there was little social interchange with ordinary Indians. Taboos existed on both sides. On the Indian side major stumbling blocks were purdah and dietary restrictions: an orthodox Hindu would not eat meat while a devout Muslim would eat meat of any kind other than pork but would not touch alcohol. The notion of white superiority was sufficient for many of the British, particularly those of the pre-1914 generation, to keep their distance. They would not travel with Indians in the same railway compartment. When walking in the

37 Home comforts. Mail Order catalogues were essential reading, espeically for those living in remote up-country areas.

bequeathed to India a uniform legal system and a system of government based on parliamentary democracy. In 1947 many felt that they were leaving a task which was only half-completed and that the final British withdrawal had been too hasty. Most realized, however, that there was no lasting place for the British in India. As one memsahib put it:

You must never take land away from people. People's land has a mystique. You can go and possibly order them about for a bit and introduce some new ideas and possibly dragoon an alien race into attitudes that are not quite familiar to them. But then you must go away and die in Cheltenham.

Vere Lady Birdwood (b. 1909)

Vere Lady Birdwood, Vere Ogilvie before her marriage in 1931, had a family connection with India which dated back to the second half of the eighteenth century. In 1765 her four-times great grandfather arrived at Fort St George in Madras, one of the earliest British settlements in India, as a writer for the East India Company. Her own grandfather served as an ICS officer in the Punjab between 1863 and 1896. Her father, Sir George Drummond Ogilvie, an army officer who joined the Indian Political Service in 1905, worked at Delhi

38 "But once you stepped inside the home, you were back in Cheltenham or Bath or wherever": the interior of a british bungalow.

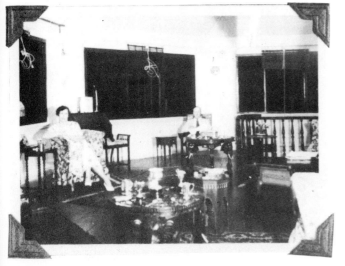

during the First World War as an official in the Army Department of the Government of India. After the war and until his retirement in 1937, he held a number of senior positions in the Political Service which included postings as British Resident in the princely states of Udaipur in Rajputana and Kashmir.

Born in England in 1909, Lady Birdwood was taken to India when only three months old. At the age of eleven, some three or four years later than usual because of the First World War, she was sent home to England to complete her education. The separation from her parents stood out as her most vivid memory. It was, as she recalled, a "traumatic experience" for a child who could think of little else for weeks before the parting actually took place. It was also a difficult period for a mother who had to decide how to divide her time between her husband in India and her children at school in England. Such separations, however, made the children independent in the sense that they became accustomed to looking after themselves from a very early age. This was particularly true in the case of Lady Birdwood's younger brother who saw his father for a mere six weeks during the six years that he spent at school in England and who used to pack his own school trunk from the age of eight.

Another of Lady Birdwood's childhood

memories was of her parents' preoccupation with the question of promotion, a concern shared by most official families in India during the early years of the twentieth century. Although they were housed, sometimes in quite exotic locations, and provided with Indian servants, these families were still dependent for their well-being and their standard of living upon the father's salary. During the early stages of his career, the salary of a junior official was not that great and most of what he earned was saved to provide for his children's education. British officials in India did not have private or independent sources of income. In consequence, if anything happened to the father, the family would have little or nothing to fall back on. This was why promotion, which went strictly according to seniority, was so important. A more senior job with a higher salary meant not only a higher standard of living but also greater security for the family.

Closely related to the question of promotion was the question of honours. Honours, according to Lady Birdwood, were the "only critical record of a successful career". An air of despondency descended upon households when the King's Birthday or the New Year's Honours were announced and the father's name was not included. The sense of disappointment was felt most keenly by the memsahib or lady of the house for whom life in India was often rather lonely. The Edwardian lady of Lady Birdwood's mother's generation was brought up to be a wife and a mother and very little else. It was the men who, in the course of their military or civilian duties, came into contact with the Indian people and who studied India's history, culture, religions and languages. The memsahib had her Indian servants but Lady Birdwood's mother, who spent 30 years in India, spoke no more than 40 or 50 words of Hindustani and "hardly knew a Hindu from a Muslim". British women were never fully integrated into India in the sense

39 Invitations to attend important state or ceremonial occasions were, like honours, of considerable importance to the higher circles of the British Raj.

This card must be shown to secure admittance to the Durbar Amphitheatre.

*Coronation Durbar
of The King Emperor
and Queen Empress
Delhi, 12th December 1911.*

Admit *Mr. A. W. ....*

to Block 9   No. 16.

Uniform full dress.
Court dress for those not entitled to wear uniform.
Morning Dress permitted where Court dress not available.
Collar Day.

*A Henry ....
Master of the Ceremonies.*

that British men were. The memsahib read good books and could run a house well, precisely what would have been expected of her had she been living in England.

The situation began to change by the time of Lady Birdwood's generation. Lady Birdwood herself developed an interest in Indian religions and philosophies. She took a course in shorthand and typing, worked as a freelance journalist and, at the beginning of the Second World War, obtained a position as a private secretary to the Governor of the province of Sind. But the lasting image is one of the memsahib recreating a little corner of England wherever she lived in India:

As regards the cultural background to our lives, I would say that in our home life we brought with us almost an exact replica, but in the context of India, of the sort of life that upper middle class people lived in England at the time. Nearly everyone in official India sprang from precisely the same educational and cultural background. From bungalow to bungalow, one found the same sort of furniture, the same sort of dinner table set, the same kind of conversation. We ate India, we drank India and we were looked after by Indian servants. . . . Some of us, particularly the younger generation and some of the men, made close studies of Indian customs, habits, philosophy, religion and so forth. But once you stepped inside the home, you were back in Cheltenham or Bath or wherever . . . (*Plain Tales from the Raj*)

Officials in India were rarely kept in the same posting for more than three years. Their families were, therefore, constantly on the move and had several homes. When she returned to India from school in England at the age of 17, Lady Birdwood's father was the Resident in the princely state of Udaipur in Rajputana. The capital, also named Udaipur, was a beautiful city of lakes and palaces. The British Residency was a converted Indian palace. With the exception of a brief period

40 Udaipur in Rajputana: "a beautiful city of lakes and palaces".

when a European doctor lived in the city, Lady Birdwood's family were the only European inhabitants. Lady Birdwood's friends, with whom she recalled playing tennis, were the descendants of the Rajput chiefs and nobles of Udaipur whose heroic exploits had become part of India's folklore.

In 1929 Lady Birdwood's father was posted as the Resident at Kashmir. In the following year she accompanied her father on an official tour which took them to Hunza and Naga, the northern-most regions of India on the borders of what was then Chinese Turkestan. The journey, along a trading route which had been used for centuries, took three months and they travelled, with their retainers, by pony and yak with mules carrying their baggage. Overnights stops were spent either in rest houses along the route or in tents. At Hunza they encountered people with red hair and blue eyes who were said to be descended from

41 British cantonment on the north-west frontier during the 1937 Waziristan campaign. The electrified barbed-wire fence gave Lady Birdwood the impression of living in a concentration camp.

the soldiers of Alexander the Great who made his way into India by the same route in 325BC

In 1931 Lady Birdwood married Christopher Birdwood, an army officer and the son of Field Marshal Birdwood, the Commander-in-Chief of the Indian army. In one respect Lady Birdwood's life did not change: she moved home 14 times in as many months. She found it difficult, however, to adjust to her new life. Having previously enjoyed so much freedom as the daughter of a political officer stationed in some of the most glamorous of India's princely states, she found life as the wife of an army officer somewhat claustrophobic. Her social contacts were now confined to her husband's regiment and she found regimental small-talk and gossip trivial and tedious. The cantonments or military stations at which the regiments were based were so alike that Lady Birdwood was convinced that she could have been anywhere in the world – Africa, the Caribbean, even Aldershot. The sense of confinement was heightened when the regiment was stationed at Bannu on the north-west frontier during the Waziristan campaign of 1937. Civilians were not permitted to go within a quarter of a mile of an electrified barbed-wire fence which surrounded the entire station. To Lady Birdwood it was almost like living in a concentration camp.

The Indian nationalist movement seldom affected Lady Birdwood or her circle of friends. As she recalled:

We were aware of the political problems but they did not impinge upon our lives in any way. If we thought about Gandhi at all it was really that he was just a bit of a nuisance and slightly absurd. It was obvious that he had a very big following in India. But beyond that we were not very much concerned with what either Gandhi or his followers were doing.

When she made vacation visits to England, usually once every three years, Lady Birdwood found such disinterest in Indian affairs that she seldom talked about India at all. Occasionally, over dinner, she might have been asked, "Well, what's all this about old Gandhi?" The manner in which the question was asked indicated that it was hardly the moment to settle down to a serious discussion about India. Lady Birdwood simply shrugged her shoulders and then felt suitably relieved when her host or hostess, or whoever had put the question, moved on to news of the latest theatre production in London.

India was home for Lady Birdwood for 35 years. It was, in her own words, "something which simply belonged to us and to all of us who lived there". She and those who shared her experience knew that one day they would leave India. But this awareness did not affect their day-to-day thinking when it seemed as if life in India would go on for ever. They never questioned their right to be there. As Lady Birdwood recalled:

I can honestly say that at the time when we were living and working in India, there was absolutely no feeling of exploitation, no feeling of being wicked imperialists. In fact in those days we did not think imperialists were necessarily wicked. We thought they were bringing enlightenment to backward parts of the world.

Kenneth Warren (1886-1983)

Kenneth Warren's family connection with the tea trade and the tea industry dated back to the first half of the nineteenth century. His grandfather on his mother's side was based at Canton in China in the 1830s buying tea on behalf of his London merchant firm.

The East India Company set up two experimental tea-gardens, or plantations, in Assam, one of which was bought in 1849 by Warren's great uncle. It was known as Chabwa (*cha* meaning tea, and *bwa* meaning a garden or plantation). Having no family of his own, the great uncle took his three nephews, one of whom was Kenneth Warren's father, into the business as apprentices. But Chabwa was not a success, and in 1877 the Warren family established the Doom Dooma Tea Company whose tea-gardens were located in one of the most remote regions of Assam near the Burmese border. As the tea industry expanded and the civil administration to run it did likewise, the Warren family also established a trading company, known as The Planters' Stores and Agency Company, which brought in supplies from Calcutta.

Living conditions for the tea-planters on the Doom Dooma estate were much better in 1906 when Kenneth Warren arrived as an assistant managerial executive than they had been during his father's time. Nonetheless, amenities for the assistants were still rather basic. They lived in bungalows which were elevated about 2 metres above the ground. Each bungalow had a timber framework and a thatched roof. The walls consisted of wooden panels which were filled with reed and earth mixed with cow dung and covered with whitewash. The ceiling consisted of hessian or sack-cloth which was also whitewashed. The space between the cloth and the thatched roof was the home of bats and, occasionally, snakes.

Warren's furniture consisted of a bed which he bought in Calcutta and two chairs which he bought in a local bazaar. He made do with

42 Kenneth Warren with his son.

43 The bungalow in which Warren lived as a senior manager on the Doom Dooma tea-garden.

inverted tea chests for a table, a chest of drawers and a wardrobe. For lighting he had a hurricane lamp and candles with beer bottles as candlesticks. For washing he had a tin "hip-bath" which was located on a cement floor beneath his bedroom. It was approached by a ladder through a trap door. The drain which let water out was also a way in for various reptiles. Returning from work on a particularly hot and sticky afternoon during the rainy season, Warren decided to take a bath. While he was in the bath he felt it moving. He looked over the side to see a large snake unwinding itself. He called his servants and they killed it. It was a python, nearly 5 metres in length.

Warren shared the bungalow with three other bachelors. There was no such thing as a married assistant: only the very senior managers were permitted to marry. Besides, young assistants could not afford to marry. Warren's starting salary was the equivalent of what would now be £2.50 a month. Initially he depended on company loans. His first pony, his means of transport around the estate, was bought with borrowed money. After three years he received a small annual commission from company profits. After a further three years he was in a position to pay off his debts. It took him six years, therefore, before he could start saving. When he retired as a senior manager 20 years later his salary was the equivalent of £33 a month. On this he could afford to keep three polo ponies (he was captain of his local polo club) and employ a "riding boy" to look after them. He could also employ a chauffeur. He was able to entertain, to go on shooting and fishing expeditions and to attend local race meetings. "On the whole", he later wrote, it was "a very pleasant and enjoyable as well as interesting life at a minimum cost". There was little or no income tax which meant that the cost of living was low. An ordinary chicken, for instance, cost a mere two *annas*, about 1p.

Conditions were very different for the tea-garden labourers, or coolies as they were known. This was particularly true during the early days of the tea industry in Assam. Then, most of Assam was virgin forest and inaccessible except by river. Roads were little more than forest tracks and the first railway was not opened until 1884. The tea-planters depended on immigrant labour which was brought in from neighbouring Bengal. Contractors were hired to supply the labourers who were herded into recruitment depots at Calcutta and then sent up river by steamer to Assam. Squalid and insanitary living conditions at the depots and on the steamers caused many deaths from cholera. Conditions were no better on the tea-gardens. Between 1863 and 1866, of 84,915 labourers recruited, no less than 30,000 died. In a single year between 1865 and 1866 over 9000 died and over 3000 deserted. The labourers were indentured, which meant that they were bound by contract to work for a specified period on the gardens to which they were recruited. If they failed to work normally or if they absconded they were liable to criminal prosecution and punishment. These "penal" contracts, together with the remoteness of Assam, meant that the tea-garden labourers were virtually prisoners.

Gradually, as a result of a number of government enquiries into recruiting methods and working conditions, the life of the tea-garden labourers began to improve. The planters themselves were brought to realize that they could only overcome their labour-shortage problems by offering more attractive living and working conditions. Penal contracts were made illegal in 1926 and, in 1931, the Royal Commission on Labour in India recommended that immigrant workers on the tea-gardens should have the right, after three years' service, to return to their homes at their employer's expense. Legislation to this effect was enacted in 1932. But there was always room for improvement. A report in 1946 by a Government of India Labour Investigation Committee, which examined labour conditions on the tea-gardens, observed that wages were still too low and that more could be done to improve education and sanitation facilities. The report also maintained:

It is no argument to say that the labourers are

better off in plantations than they would have been in their home villages as this only amounts to exploiting their economic weakness. That they are seemingly happy is also no argument as this happiness is based on their ignorance of anything better and on their helplessness to improve their lot.

According to Kenneth Warren, Doom Dooma, which was noted for its maternity benefits, pregnant women being given three months' paid leave before and after childbirth, was like a large family. The planters represented parental authority and the labourers were said to be their respectful children. Labourers wanting a special concession or making a request were required to salaam and say, "Your Honour, you Sir are my Mother and my Father." The relationship was actually known as the *Ma-Bap* or mother-father system. Warren's view of the British Raj was based on the same system. He believed that the majority of the Indian people were happy and contented and and that they accepted British rule because it provided justice, law and order and "reasonable

prosperity". Recalling his experiences as a tea-planter in Assam he wrote:

The British in those days being the ruling race expected and received a certain standard of courtesy and politeness. There were certain rules of polite procedure shown towards both the British and upper-class Indians, which a lower- or middle-class Indian was expected to follow, such as closing his umbrella, which he used as a sunshade, when speaking to or passing a European or, if riding his pony, he was expected to dismount and lead the pony when passing on the road. (K. Warren, *Tea Tales of Assam*)

Before he left India in 1926 Warren served for two years as an elected representative of the European business community in the legislative assembly of Assam. He then became a director in London of the Planters' Stores and Agency Company which changed its name in 1949 to James Warren and Company. He was Chairman and Managing Director between 1951 and 1966. Until his retirement in 1969, he was also Chairman and Managing Director of the Warren group of tea and other companies. Doom Dooma, owned by the Warren family since 1877, was taken over by Brooke Bond in 1964.

44 Warren (seated second left) with other managers and labourers at Doom Dooma.

Charles Freer Andrews (1871-1940)

Affectionately known to his close friends as "Charlie" or "CFA", Charles Freer Andrews went to India as a missionary in 1904 at the age of 33. He joined the staff of St Stephen's College in Delhi which was run by an educational body known as the Cambridge Mission. What little he knew about India when he first arrived was derived almost entirely from his childhood. Recalling, years later, his own father's enthusiasm for the Empire, he wrote:

I never heard one single word of blame with regard to British rule in India. The idea was always impressed on me that it was the most glorious event in the whole of British history and unique in the history of the world. ("Biographical Notes", D. O'Connor [ed.] *The Testimony of C.F. Andrews*)

The reality for Andrews was somewhat different. He rapidly formed his own conclusion that British rule in India was based on little more than white domination and racial discrimination. To his dismay, he found that the same applied to the church. Andrews' philosophy as a missionary was based on the words of Jesus: "I come not to destroy but to fulfil". In other words, the object was not to destroy Hinduism or any other Indian religion but to interpret them in terms of the Christian message. He described his missionary colleagues as "noble-minded men", but found that on missionary subjects "they were almost one and all narrowly bigoted". Reflecting on the missionary outlook at the turn of the century he wrote in 1921:

I hardly ever heard anything really good about the people of India from them . . . all sorts of stories, not of the intellectual dullness but of the moral obliquity [having no moral standards] of the Indian people, stories of the treatment of Indian women, the treatment of depressed classes, treatment of widows, etc., which I have

45 C.F. Andrews.

since found to be altogether one-sided . . . . My ideas of India were confused. On the one hand I had been told about the greatness of the Hindu past and about the Islamic civilisation, but this was represented to me as almost entirely overgrown by corruption. I would emphasise the fact that it was the missionary picture which gave the most dark view. . . . The missionary view of Hinduism was almost entirely destructive.

This prejudiced missionary view was to be found even within the Cambridge Mission. Andrews fought an uphill struggle before finally overcoming the opposition to the appointment of an Indian as a new Principal of St Stephen's College.

46 The Debating Society at St Stephen's College, Delhi, in 1914-15. Andrews is fourth from the left on the second row up.

Andrews dedicated his life to combating racial prejudice in whatever form it appeared and to promoting racial harmony and understanding. His views brought him an ever-increasing circle of Indian friends. In 1906 he was invited to attend the annual session of the Indian National Congress which was held at Calcutta. Increasingly he began to identify with Indian cultural, political and religious ideas. Although he remained a Christian he left the priesthood in 1914. He had already begun to see India as the cradle of a universal religion which preached the brotherhood of man regardless of colour or race. He paid frequent visits to his family and friends in England but he now regarded India as his home and Indians as his fellow-countrymen.

Of all his Indian associates, two were particularly important. The first was Rabindranath Tagore, the Bengali poet who received the Nobel Prize for Literature in

47 Andrews (left) with a missionary friend and Gandhi in South Africa in 1914.

1913 and who was honoured with a knighthood in 1915. Andrews was drawn to Tagore like a magnet. The two men shared an identical quest: a meeting of minds to bring east and west together in love and harmony. In 1901 Tagore founded Santiniketan, the "Abode of Peace", at Bolpur near Calcutta. Santiniketan was both an *ashram*, or spiritual retreat, and a teaching college. Andrews was a regular visitor at Santiniketan and it became one of his homes in India after he had left the priesthood.

Gandhi was the second Indian of particular importance to Andrews. When Andrews arrived in India in 1904, Gandhi had been in South Africa for 11 years. Gandhi had quickly discovered that South Africa was a country run for and by white men; blacks and browns were treated as second-class citizens. A victim himself of racial prejudice, Gandhi took up the cause of the Indian community, which totalled about 100,000 at the outbreak of the First World War. The majority were indentured labourers who worked either on the coffee, tea and sugar plantations or in the gold and diamond mines. Gandhi had gone to South Africa, initially for a year, to represent an Indian merchant in a lawsuit. He decided to stay on and, in time, abandoned his lucrative legal practice and the comfortable lifestyle to which he had become accustomed. He disciplined himself to accept a life of simplicity and established settlements which became experiments in community living. He also developed his strategy of *satyagraha* which some referred to as passive resistance but which Gandhi himself described as truth or soul-force. The idea was to oppose unjust laws, not by violent protest, but by deliberately breaking them in a peaceful manner and inviting the penalty for so doing. By displaying a willingness to undergo personal suffering, Gandhi believed that, in time, the law-enforcer would come to accept the justice of the law breaker's cause. Gandhi was arrested on three occasions in South Africa. He once appeared in court with handcuffs on his wrists and manacles on his feet. In prison he was set to work breaking stones.

In 1913 in India an appeal was launched for support and funds to help Gandhi in South Africa. Charlie Andrews was one of the first to respond. He sailed for Durban and landed in January 1914. After a few days he wrote to a friend in India:

Mr Gandhi is not really fighting for this privilege or that; he is fighting for the right to be called men not slaves.

Andrews by this time was more than just a missionary. His own outspoken views had brought him contacts in high places. He was a personal friend of the Viceroy, Lord Hardinge. The Viceroy had been seriously injured in an assassination attempt in 1912 and Andrews had provided much needed comfort to Hardinge and his family. Andrews exercised considerable influence over Hardinge to the extent that he almost became the Viceroy's conscience. Andrews was not, therefore, overawed by the authorities in South Africa. He acted as a mediator between Gandhi and General Smuts, the South African Prime Minister. An agreement was reached which conceded some of Gandhi's demands, but Indians continued to be the victims of racial prejudice and discrimination. For Andrews, his first meeting with Gandhi had been like a scene from the New Testament. He knelt before Gandhi and touched his feet. Gandhi replied in a soft voice: "Pray do not do that; it is a humiliation to me."

Having seen the conditions under which the Indian community lived in South Africa, Andrews proceeded to launch what was an almost single-handed crusade on behalf of Indian communities living and working in other countries. He first turned his attention to Fiji and the Indian indentured labourers who worked on the sugar plantations. He visited Fiji in 1915 and produced a report which condemned the "moral degradation" which resulted from the indenture system. Hardinge was impressed by the report; so much so that in a speech to the Imperial Legislative Council in 1916 he committed the Government of India to the abolition of the overseas indenture system. A law to this effect was passed in 1920. Much of the credit must go to Charlie Andrews.

Any sense of elation Andrews may have felt over the abolition of overseas indenture was shattered in 1920 when he became aware of the magnitude of the events surrounding the massacre at Amritsar. He was determined to see for himself what had happened and was appalled by what he found. He was introduced to a village headman, a Sikh who had served as a soldier during the First World War, who had been accused of being involved in acts of sabotage on the railways. When he denied all knowledge of the sabotage he was flogged in public. As with Gandhi, Andrews stooped down and touched the feet of the headman; he asked him to forgive the British for their evil-doing. Andrews was incensed. He believed now that India would have to sever her link with Britain to achieve her independence. There could be no independence for India within the British Empire. "In such an Empire", he wrote, "there is only one place for an Asiatic, and that is an inferior place." In arguing along these lines he went further even than Gandhi, who believed that it might still be possible to maintain the British connection if the British could be brought to realize the error of their ways.

In subsequent years Andrews did soften his position. He preached the cause of reconciliation between Britain and India but never ceased to emphasize that the relationship would have to be one of complete equality, with India being allowed to work out her own destiny. "In the present situation", he wrote in 1935, "the British Parliament acts the part of Pharaoh and Gandhi has to act the part of Moses." At the same time, he continued his campaigns on behalf of Indian communities abroad, particularly those in South Africa. He died in Calcutta in April 1940 at the age of 69. Gandhi's tribute to him has become his epitaph:

I want Englishmen and Indians, whilst the memory of this servant of England and India is still fresh, to give a thought to the legacy he has left for us both. . . . At the present moment I do not wish to think of English misdeeds. They will be forgotten, but not one of the heroic deeds of Andrews will be forgotten so long as England and India live. If we really love Andrews' memory we may not have hate in us for Englishmen, of whom Andrews was among the best and noblest. It is possible, quite possible, for the best Englishmen and the best Indians to meet together and never to separate till they have evolved a formula acceptable to both. The legacy left by Andrews is worth the effort. (Quoted in Hugh Tinker, *The Ordeal of Love: C.F. Andrews and India*)

PRINCES, PARTITION AND ANGLO-INDIANS

This section looks first at the relations between the British and an Indian prince and considers how the prince responded to the independence movement. It looks also at the experiences of a Muslim policeman in the Punjab at the time of partition. Finally, an Anglo-Indian nurse tells what life in India was like for the Anglo-Indian community.

Just under a third of India was never brought under direct British rule. This was the territory of over 500 princely states. Although responsible for the government of their states, none of the princes, no matter what their rank or importance, could regard themselves as independent. They owed allegiance to the British Crown and they came under the jurisdiction of the Political Department of the Government of India. A handful of princes were pioneers in the field of social and economic reform but politically they were all conservative and autocratic. As such, the British regarded the princes as their natural allies in the struggle against the democratic nationalists of British India.

When independence came in 1947 the princes were advised to join either India or

48 The Chamber of Princes in 1929. Maharaja Ganga Singh of Bikaner is standing behind the Viceroy, Lord Irwin.

Pakistan. The majority did so but the rulers of the two most important – Hyderabad and Kashmir – refused. In both cases religion was a complicating factor. In Hyderabad a Muslim prince ruled over a population which was predominantly Hindu; in Kashmir the reverse was the case. Hyderabad was occupied by India in September 1948 and annexed. Over Kashmir, hostilities broke out in October 1947 with both India and Pakistan claiming the territory as their own. A cease-fire line, arranged by the United Nations in 1949, has since become a permanent frontier.

For the majority of Indians, particularly the peasants, life under British rule went on much as before. They were, of course, affected by various aspects of British policy. Gandhi never ceased to protest about what he regarded as the main economic consequences of British rule. On the eve of the salt march he wrote to Lord Irwin:

49 The partition of India and the movement of refugees, 1947.

And why do I regard British rule in India as a curse? It has impoverished the dumb millions by a system of progressive exploitation and by a ruinously expensive military and civil administration which the country can never afford.

Gandhi also complained that the burden of taxation, on commodities such as salt, drugs and drink, fell heaviest on the poor whose main means of subsistence, hand-spun cotton goods made in the village, had been undermined by the import of Lancashire textiles. It was not always easy to convey this message to the Indian people because, as Rashid Ali Baig, a former Indian member of the ICS observed, most of them had other preoccupations:

Britain never encouraged Indian industry. Britain was really a large factory. It took wheat from India, turned it into biscuits and sent them back to India. It took cotton from India, turned it into cloth and sent it back to India. But the

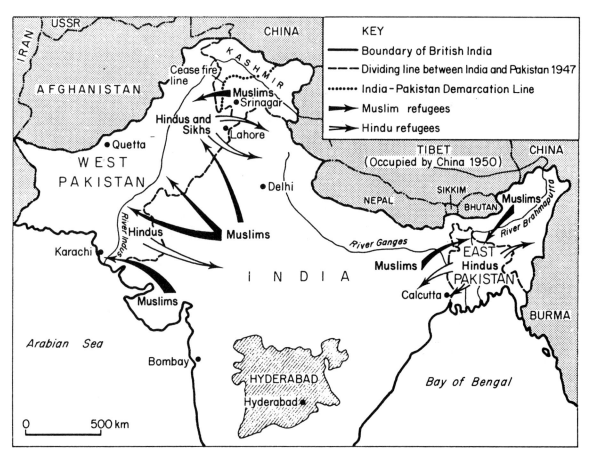

average Indian never thought in terms of India and Britain. He thought of his own problems, where his bread for the next day would come from.

Independence in 1947 was generally greeted with ecstatic celebrations, but not by everyone. For a number of Anglo-Indians who regarded themselves as British and India as their home, the future now seemed uncertain. For millions of Hindus, Muslims and Sikhs, the partition of India became a nightmare. The political deadlock between Congress and the Muslim League was finally broken at the beginning of June 1947 when the leaders on both sides gave their consent to Mountbatten's partition plan. Mountbatten then announced that British rule would come to an end on 15 August. Speed was essential in the Viceroy's view to prevent any possibility of a breakdown. There remained 10 weeks in which to make the necessary arrangements. The armed forces and the civil services had to be divided; so too did India's financial assets and liabilities. Above all, the boundary lines had to be drawn in Bengal and the Punjab. For this purpose a Boundary Commission was appointed. A British judge presided as Chairman over a Commission consisting of four Indian judges, two appointed by Congress and two by the Muslim League. As the Commission deliberated, the Sikhs of the Punjab made it clear that they would oppose by force any decision that they considered unjust. Passions exploded on all sides in the Punjab when the award of the Boundary Commission was announced on 16 August. In the ensuing weeks and months, as people tried desperately to move themselves, their families and their belongings to the right side of the boundary line, an estimated 200,000 were killed and over 11 million became refugees. Similarly, on the other side of India, when East Bengal became East Pakistan, over a million Hindus migrated from the east to West Bengal which remained as part of India. Whether more could have been done to prevent the carnage and whether the whole process of partition had been rushed through too quickly, are subjects which have been endlessly debated since 1947. Whatever the case, in terms of the lives lost and the disruption caused, the partition of India remains one of the great human tragedies of the twentieth century.

Ganga Singh (1880-1943)

Bikaner was the second largest princely state in Rajputana. The state took its name from its founder, Beekar, who, in 1485, established a small fort at a spot called Nera in the middle of the Indian desert. Hence Beekar-Nera – Bikaner. Bikaner had enjoyed a distinguished history under the Mughals. Marriage alliances were established with the Mughal court and successive rulers of Bikaner had served the Mughal emperors either as military commanders or as civilian governors. In 1818, in the wake of the decline of the Mughal empire, Bikaner signed a treaty of alliance with the British. The state pledged its loyalty to the British and received in return guarantees of its internal and external security. The ruler of Bikaner sided with the British during the Great Revolt of 1857. When the revolt was over he received a personal message from Queen Victoria expressing gratitude for his "loyalty and devotion".

Ganga Singh, the twenty-first ruler of Bikaner, was born in 1880. He succeeded as Maharaja when he was only seven. Until he came of age, Bikaner was governed by a Council of Regency which had a British official as its President. Between 1890 and 1895 Ganga Singh was educated at the Mayo College at Ajmer in Rajputana. The Mayo College was one of a number of colleges which the British had established to provide future Indian princes with all that was best in an English public school education. As befitted a young Rajput prince, Ganga Singh followed up his time at college with a spell of military training as a cadet in a regiment of the Indian army. Under the watchful eye of an English tutor and guardian appointed by the Government of India, he then received his administrative training in preparation for the time when he would himself assume the reins of government. Eventually, in 1898 at the age of 18, Ganga Singh was invested with his ruling powers.

Like his predecessors, Ganga Singh was intensely loyal to the British Crown. During the famine of 1899-1900, when the desert state of Bikaner was hit particularly badly, Ganga Singh personally supervised relief operations. Canals were dug to provide irrigation. The revenue payments of the peasants were suspended and they were provided with loans. Relief works and famine camps were established. Priority was given to the construction of a railway which provided a vital communication link with the Punjab. For his part in the relief operations, Ganga Singh received the Kaiser-i-Hind medal, first class, which was awarded by the British for particularly notable acts of public service. The Maharaja also achieved military distinction in the service of the British Empire. He fought in China in 1900-1 at the head of the famous Bikaner Imperial Service Camel Corps and again in Somaliland in East Africa in 1903. For his services in China he was made a Knight Commander of the Indian Empire. In 1902 he was one of two Indian princes who represented Rajputana at the coronation in London of King Edward VII. He was appointed Aide-de-Camp to the Prince of Wales and became an honorary major in the Indian army. In 1904, in recognition of the part played by his Camel Corps in Somaliland,

50 Maharaja Ganga Singh of Bikaner in 1903, aged 23.

he became a Knight Commander of the Most Exalted Order of the Star of India. He served in France and Egypt during the First World War. In 1917 he represented the princes of India at the Imperial War Cabinet and Conference in London. At the end of the war, he was chosen as a member of the delegation which represented India at the peace conference in Paris. He was the first Chancellor of a Chamber of Princes which was established in 1921 and, at the beginning of the 1930s, he was one of the leading princely delegates at the Round Table Conferences in London.

Sauve and sophisticated, speaking English and French as if they were his own languages,

51 The palace at Bikaner.

52 March past of the Bikaner Imperial Camel Corps.

Ganga Singh elevated snobbery and etiquette almost to an art form. He once criticized the wife of a Viceroy for having eaten cheese off her knife. Constantly striving to emulate his British overlords, he spared no expense in providing elaborate ceremonial welcomes and lavish entertainments for his distinguished British visitors. Lord Irwin described his arrival at Bikaner in February 1927 in a letter to his father:

We left Delhi on last Tuesday afternoon and travelled in a funny little train up a metre-guage line to Bikaner, which we reached the following morning at half-past nine. There we were met with great pomp and, after all the business at the station was over – of being introduced to people and inspecting guards of honour and so on – we drove up to the Palace escorted by the Bikaner Camel Corps. You never saw anything so odd, as the camels look ambling along at about seven miles an hour with their noses very high in the air. The morning was more or less spent in further

ceremonials and ended up with my formal visit to the Maharaja, which took place in the old Fort. It was a rather fine hall – oblong shaped, red sandstone – and was filled with all the Maharaja's nobles and important people in beautiful clothes; and after he had met me at the door, we progressed up the middle preceded by our respective staffs and then made formal conversation for a moment or two, after which his principal nobles were presented. All this being finished, we went away again. It was quite one of the best ceremonial things I have yet seen; the colour of the hall, the colour of the clothes was all very good.

The principal entertainment was the shooting of the Bikaner imperial sandgrouse, a bird found nowhere else in the world. Every

53 "Every British official in India, from the Viceroy to the District Officer, was expected to be a good shot": Lord Reading (centre), Viceroy 1921-6, at the end of a hunting expedition in the princely state of Udaipur.

British official in India, from the Viceroy to the District Officer, was expected to be a good shot. In order to shoot sandgrouse at Bikaner the guests would assemble at Gujner, a palace some 18 miles outside the capital on the shores of an artificial lake. For three days beforehand the birds were kept away from the lake by the Maharaja's servants. When eventually they were allowed to quench their thirst they were shot in their hundreds. They were boiled in oil to remove the skin as well as the feathers and then served as a great delicacy at a sumptuous state banquet.

Ganga Singh believed that an autocratic system of government, in which he personally was the sole source of authority, was best-suited to the interests of his state and to the needs of his subjects. He had little time for the nationalist movement in British India. He regarded the nationalist demand for self-government as being nothing but disloyal. Equally, he viewed the successive stages by

54 Ganga Singh escorts the Prince of Wales into the palace at Bikaner during the royal tour of India, 1921-2.

which the British introduced political reforms in India as being nothing but dangerous. To Ganga Singh these reforms were playing into the hands of radical agitators who increasingly criticized the princes as being little more than puppets of the imperial government. In short, in common with many of the other princes, Ganga Singh was not prepared to surrender his powers in order to become a constitutional figurehead like the monarch in Britain. He did, in 1913, permit the establishment of a Representative Assembly in Bikaner but he made it clear at the time that this would be only an advisory body and would not exercise real power.

The British, for their part, were not inclined to persuade the princes to associate their subjects more closely with the government of their states. Increasingly during the twentieth century the British regarded the princes as their only dependable allies against the nationalist movement in British India. Under these circumstances the British were hardly likely to induce the princes to adopt the sort of reforms that they themselves were so hesitant about introducing in British India. Nonetheless, as Lord Irwin admitted to his father in 1927, there was bound to be trouble if the gap between British India and princely India became too wide:

I think they [the princes] are getting rather uneasy now about their future, and public opinion is beginning to play on them a little bit in the matter of the rudiments of administration and government; but only very slowly, and the trouble is that political consciousness on these elementary matters is progressing so much faster in British India than it is in their territories, that some sort of clash is every day, I think, coming a little closer.

A handful of princes, of whom Ganga Singh was one of the most prominent, attempted to devise safeguards whereby they could protect themselves against the nationalist movement. Increasingly, they put their faith in the legal argument that they had treaties with the British which guaranteed them protection in the face of threats to their security. They argued that it would be a breach of faith if the British deserted them. This was an increasingly unrealistic position to adopt. The princes were the last to realize that a treaty can be maintained only so long as the parties concerned possess both the will and the power to enforce it. By the end of the Second World War the British knew that they would not be in a position to protect the princes beyond Indian independence.

Ganga Singh died in 1943 at the age of 63. His son and heir, Sadul Singh, was much more realistic in reading the signs of the times. When it became clear in 1947 that the British were going, Bikaner, under the guidance of Sadul Singh, became one of the first of the princely states to throw in its lot with the new Indian government.

Mohammed Ibrahim

When India and Pakistan became independent in August 1947 Mohammed Ibrahim was working as a Sub-Inspector of Police in the Karnal district of the Amabala Division of the the Punjab. Karnal was situated in East Punjab. It was bordered in the east by the United Provinces and in the west by the princely states of the Punjab. According to the census of 1941, the last taken before independence, Karnal had a total population of just under 995,000. Of these just over 666,000 were non-Muslims, mainly Hindus and Sikhs, and nearly 286,000 were Muslims. There was never any question, therefore, that when the boundary line was drawn in 1947 Karnal, as part of East Punjab, would be awarded to India. As a Muslim policeman in an area which was now part of India, Mohammed Ibrahim had a choice. He could either remain where he was or request a transfer to West Punjab which became part of Pakistan after 15 August 1947.

Unlike those districts of the Punjab which were either adjacent to or dissected by the boundary line which was drawn in August 1947, Karnal had enjoyed a relatively peaceful existence in the months and weeks preceding independence. The districts of Lahore, Amritsar and Gurdaspur had been the scene of savage inter-communal fighting. On 10 July

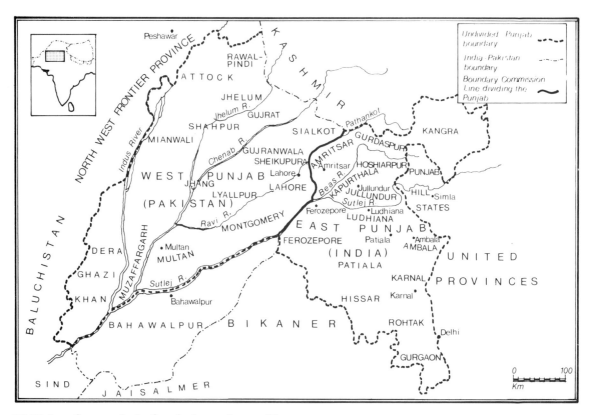

55 Partition of the Punjab, 1947.

1947, just five weeks before independence, Sir Evan Jenkins, the outgoing British governor of the Punjab, reported to Lord Mountbatten that everyone was behaving "as though they had just been at war and were going to have a new war within a few weeks". As a precautionary measure against the outbreak of violence on a much greater scale when the award of the Boundary Commission was announced, a Punjab Boundary Force was established at the beginning of August 1947 and stationed in those districts where the most serious trouble was expected. As the violence escalated Jenkins bombarded Mountbatten with telegrams to the effect that the Boundary Force was inadequate. Reinforcements were sent but even then the Boundary Force could not cope. On the eve of independence Field Marshal Sir Claude Auchinleck, the last British Commander-in-Chief of the Indian army, flew over the trouble spots and reported that "no amount of troops can stop the indiscriminate butchery which appears to be going on on both sides".

The inadequacy of the Punjab Boundary Force was not the only headache for Jenkins during his last few weeks in office. On more than one occasion he reported to Mountbatten that the police were taking sides and that they had become totally unreliable. A new Hindu Superintendent of Police arrived at Amritsar at the beginning of August. He immediately disarmed the Muslim members of the police. He had acted without approval from higher authority and he was soon suspended. Nonetheless, his action had created near panic amongst the Muslim members of the Police. They were, as Jenkins reported to Mountbatten, "anxious for their own safety and for that of their families". Many were on the point of deserting but they were told by the authorities waiting to take over in West Punjab that they would not be employed in Pakistan if they did so. At the time it was thought that Muslim policemen in East Punjab would be needed to reassure the local Muslim population.

Supreme Commander-.

Note on situation in Punjab Boundary Force Area
for the Joint Defence Council.
----

1.   I visited Lahore on the 14th August on my way back to
Delhi from Karachi and discussed the situation at length with
Sir Evan Jenkins and Major-General Rees, the Commander of the
Punjab Boundary Force.

My conclusions are set out in the following paragraphs
and represent my personal opinion based on my conversations at
Lahore and intelligence reports received in the last week or
ten days.

2.   Amritsar and vicinity.   The strife here was started by
the Sikhs who have formed armed bands of considerable strength
which are carrying out raids on Muslim or preponderantly
Muslim villages.   Three or four such raids have been occurring
nightly.   These bands are well organised and often include
mounted men who are used as scouts to reconnoitre for a
favourable opportunity.

One such band is reliably reported to have killed 200
Muslims in one village a few days ago.   The connivance of
subjects of Sikh states is strongly suspected.

There are also Muslim bands organised for the same
purpose, but these are fewer in number, smaller in size and
less well organised apparently.

The Army has had some successful encounters with some of
these bands and has caused considerable casualties in some
instances where bands have been caught red handed.   The difficulty is always of course to catch the offenders in the act as
lethal weapons can not be used against apparently peaceful
villagers unless these obstruct or themselves attack the troops
as has happened in some cases.

Constant and continuous patrolling is being carried out,
but the area is large and the troops are relatively few in
relation to it.   There is no remedy for this, unless the
troops are permanently posted in villages as armed police and
this is neither practicable or desirable.

In Amritsar City the casualties (predominantly Muslim
apparently) were high and largely due to the emasculation of
the City Police force by the disarming by a new Superintendent
of Police of the Muslim members of it.   This has since been
rectified and the official replaced.   Several houses were
burning in Amritsar City as I flew over it and four or five
villages within ten or fifteen miles of the City were
apparently completely destroyed by fire and still burning.
The Army is occupying the City in some strength.

3.   Lahore.   The aggression here is chiefly by Muslims, said
to be in retaliation for the massacring of Muslims in Amritsar.
The most disturbing feature here is the defection of the Police,
particularly the special Police, who are predominantly Muslim.
There is very strong evidence that the Police are taking little
notice of the orders of their officers (all the remaining
European officers left yesterday) and that they have actually
joined hands with the rioters in certain instances.

But for the presence of the Army there would by now be a
complete holocaust in the City.   Local Muslim leaders are
trying to persuade the Muslim soldiers to follow the bad

56   Field Marshal Auchinleck, Commander-in-Chief
of the Indian Army, reports on the situation in the
Punjab Boundary Force area, 14 August 1947.

Mohammed Ibrahim remained at his post at Karnal until 3 September 1947 when he was relieved by a Hindu Sub-Inspector of Police. He was transferred to Police Lines, that part of the district where the police were quartered, where he met a number of other Muslim policemen who had also been relieved. The Muslim officers were told to hand in their uniforms and revolvers and to vacate police quarters. Mohammed Ibrahim stayed in the town of Karnal until 21 September when, along with his colleagues, he was taken by truck to the Police Lines at Ambala on the first stage of his journey to West Punjab. For want of transport he had to leave behind most of his belongings and household effects. On 22 September he boarded a train at Ambala. He had with him his wife, who was pregnant, and his children – two boys and two girls. He also took a few boxes containing clothes, ornaments and some money. Fellow police officers from Karnal with their families travelled by the same train which had a small Hindu military escort. The train travelled first across the territory of the princely state of Patiala. What follows is Mohammed Ibrahim's account of the journey:

We were told that Patiala State territory was full of danger for travellers both by rail and road, but the train was fortunate in covering this part of the journey without mishap. However, at about five in the evening just outside Ludhiana our train stopped without reason. I noticed about sixteen armed Sikhs emerging from the bushes and advancing towards the train. They signalled and shouted to others to follow them. In a moment hundreds of Sikhs armed with swords, spears and fire-arms attacked the train. The attack was wholesale and covered the train from one end to the other. My compartment was attacked by a group of armed Sikhs who used swords and spears indiscriminately on men, women and children. My youngest son and three-year old daughter were torn to death. My two other children were seriously wounded. My wife, who was seven months' pregnant, was furiously pressed on the belly resulting in an abortion a few hours later. I was knocked down and a number of corpses fell over my body. I was

helpless and unarmed and could not help my family. My boxes containing valuables were taken by the attackers. I was the only individual who remained unhurt. There were only a few survivors of this attack, but none unhurt. The whole of the compartment was thoroughly looted. Clothes were taken from both men and women irrespective of whether they were dead or alive. This went on for about two hours. The train started only when nobody was left to kill and there was nothing left to loot. (*Disturbances in East Punjab and Contiguous Area During and After 1947*)

The military escort had been hopelessly outnumbered but Mohammed Ibrahim believed that they had not even put up a "sham fight". At Ludhiana troops were used to help the handful of survivors and to unload the dead bodies. Mohammed Ibrahim's wife and two surviving children were admitted to the Ludhiana Memorial Hospital. After five days road transport was arranged to take Mohammed Ibrahim and his family through Ferozepore and across the border to the safety of Lahore in West Punjab which was now part of Pakistan.

Mohammed Ibrahim made a statement which was published, along with many others by Muslims who had been through similar experiences, by the government of Pakistan in 1948. He explained that his wife and two children were still in a "precarious condition". He also explained that his parents had been left behind at Amritsar in India. Whether he ever saw them again is not known. Mohammed Ibrahim was one of several thousand refugees caught up in the partition holocaust in the Punjab in 1947. Muslims were by no means the only victims. Thousands of Hindus and Sikhs travelling in the opposite direction met a similar fate.

57 Muslim refugees occupy every available space on board a train waiting to take them to Pakistan from Delhi, September 1947.

Irene Edwards (b. 1906)

Irene Edwards, Irene Green before her marriage in 1938, was born in India in 1906. She was one of three daughters of an Anglo-Indian family. Her mother was the daughter of a Hindu and a Portuguese veterinary surgeon in the Bombay cavalry. Her father, who was of Scottish ancestry, was brought up in a Scottish orphanage in Secunderabad in Southern India. Like many Anglo-Indians, Irene's father worked on the Indian railways. He was attached to the army and was thus frequently posted to garrison stations. Irene was brought up in these garrison stations, or railway colonies as they were sometimes known. Her early education came from her mother who taught the three sisters how to read from the Bible. When she was about 14 Irene was sent to a railway school where she was educated up to the equivalent of primary level. Her parents could not afford to send their children to a secondary school. Her father died in 1923 when Irene was 17 and the family were very poor because her father's Provident Fund, or pension, did not amount to very much. Her mother had to leave the railway colony and search for cheap lodging places. At the age of 19, with the family finances becoming even more serious, Irene applied for a job as a trainee nurse at St George's Hospital in Bombay. She wrote what she described as a "pathetic" letter to the matron and considered herself very fortunate to have been given the job because her education was below the standard normally required.

58 Nursing in India.

Irene had never before been to a big city like Bombay. Having spent her childhood in remote up-country railway colonies, mainly in Central India, she was, by her own admission, "bewildered" when she first arrived at the hospital in Bombay. Her first uniform was made from old tennis dresses which her mother had obtained from the wives of army officers. At first she was terrified of lifts and telephones. She had neither seen nor used either of them before. She walked through the wards with her head down because she could not bear to look at the male patients in their pyjamas. The other nurses, who seemed so sophisticated by comparison, teased her unmercifully and made fun of her initials and surname – I.M. Green.

In 1929, by which time she had qualified, Irene took a job as a nursing sister at the Lady Reading Hospital in Peshawar on the north-west frontier. She arrived at a time when the frontier was living up to its troubled and unsettled reputation. British troops were involved in a campaign against the Afridis, a frontier tribe. At one stage the nursing sisters came under fire when they were taking refuge in a British cantonment. Irene and her colleagues were subsequently awarded the Frontier Medal. In 1930 Peshawar itself was gripped by riots when the "Red Shirts", a Muslim organization which supported the Indian National Congress, mounted a civil disobedience movement. Irene was again caught up in the drama. A British army officer was murdered in the hospital. Irene had been drinking coffee and arranging a golf lesson with him only moments before. She assumed that an Indian orderly, who appeared with blood pouring down his arm, had tried to help the officer. The orderly turned out to be the murderer.

Life for Anglo-Indians in India was often difficult and sometimes cruel. The offspring of mixed marriages were never fully accepted by either the British or the Indians. As a child Irene recalled that there were benches marked "Europeans only" and "Indians only". Similar signs were hung outside waiting rooms at railway stations. As an Anglo-Indian Irene never knew which one to occupy. Anglo-Indians were the targets of cruel jokes which came from both sides. Iris Portal, the daughter of a British provincial governor, recalled:

When I was very young I took the conventional attitude which everybody took – even enlightened people like my parents – of making jokes about "blackie-whites".

It was not until the Second World War, when she nursed at a hospital in Delhi and became friendly with the wife of an Anglo-Indian doctor, that Iris Portal realized, with a sense of shame, "what nonsense it all was". According to Irene Edwards, Indians looked down on Anglo-Indians because to them they were neither one thing nor the other:

Registered No. M-11.

THE

ANGLO-INDIAN

The Journal of the Anglo-Indian Association
OF
Southern India, Limited.

" SELF-HELP "   " FOUNDED, OCTOBER 7th, 1879 "

Vol. XVI.   MADRAS, MARCH, 1923.   No. 3.

A REFERENDUM

The President invites the particular attention of *every* member of our Association to page 4 *et seq* where appears in full Lieutenant-Colonel Gidney's speech on " The Indianisation of the Indian Army," to Mr. T. Rangachariar's reply, and the latter's kindly reference to Mr. D. S. White, the founder of our Association.

Colonel Gidney writes that the Government of India are not prepared to grant his request *without having before them the views of the Community*. Colonel Gidney is, therefore particularly anxious to obtain our opinion on the following specific point. " Do we desire to be treated as Indians which will make us eligible to be nominated for King's Cadetships at Sandhurst and to be admitted for training to the Preparatory College at Dehra Dhun ; or do we desire to be treated as Europeans which will allow us at present to compete by open competition at Sandhurst."

Mr. T. Rangachariar puts the problem in a nutshell when he says " Let him ask the question, 'Am I an Indian, or am I a European ?'. He must answer it himself. It depends upon his community."

The President adopts one method of broad casting through our Journal the above question to every member, and asks every member to reply. If our views are to be worthy of consideration every member must reply either one way or the other. It will be futile to communicate the replies of any number less than five hundred.

Will every member, therefore, please send a post card to the General Secretary stating " Indian " or " European " and sign his name. We shall publish the general result of this plebiscite in our next issue by giving the figures for each, but no names.

H. Y. NECKER,
President.

March 15, 1923.

59 A question of identity: "Am I an Indian, or am I a European?"

60 Garden-party at a British club in Madras. Each club had its own membership rules. High-born and well-educated Indians were sometimes admitted; Anglo-Indians hardly ever.

They used to call us *kutcha butcha*, that is to say, half-baked bread, and depending on the shade of your colour they used to talk about the Anglo-Indians as being *teen pao*, three-quarters, or *adha seer*, half a pound, if you were nearly white. (*Plain Tales from the Raj*)

Irene herself gradually became accepted but at times it was a painful experience. As a nursing sister on the frontier, working with five other sisters and a matron who were all English, Irene had to overcome the "terrible handicap" of a *chee-chee* (a sing-song) accent and "country-bred" manners. She had to learn not to say "Pleased to meet you" but instead to bow and say "How do you do?". She had to learn to say "Goodbye" and not "Cheerio" or "Chin-chin". She also had to face the supposed test of mixed blood:

I remember a young subaltern coming up to me and asking me to open my mouth. I didn't know what he was after, but he looked at my gums and then inspected my fingernails. Later on I was told that this young man was looking for the tell-tale blue gums and blue marks in the fingernails found in people of mixed races.

Anglo-Indians for the most part kept to themselves. Apart from work, their only point of contact with the British community was an occasional social function, like a dance, organized at a Railway Institute, an Anglo-Indian club. Irene was able to escape this closed society but others were less fortunate. As a frequent guest at a British social club in Peshawar, Irene tried to gain admission for one of her Anglo-Indian girlfriends. She approached a lady doctor who had influence but her friend was turned down because it was known that she was an Anglo-Indian. When Irene, who had a fairer complexion than most Anglo-Indians, pointed out that she too was an Anglo-Indian, the doctor replied, "Yes, but people don't know it here. You have passed in the crowd, but Celia won't".

Mixed marriages were frowned upon from the British point of view, but it was the unwritten rule for a young Anglo-Indian girl to try and marry a British soldier. Irene's sister married a soldier but Irene herself married an Englishman who was the manager of a mill owned by the Dunlop Rubber Company which was based near Calcutta in Bengal. They had two children, a boy and a girl. The family visited England in 1945, returned to India in 1947 when Irene's mother died and then settled permanently in England in 1950. Irene never knew her relatives in England on her father's side. India's independence in 1947 left many Anglo-Indians uncertain as to where their loyalties and identities lay. As Irene herself recalled:

We were proud of being British. My father, when he heard "God Save the King" being sung, even away in the distance, stood up and we had to stand up with him. That is what we thought of the British Raj and it came as a shock to us when it ended. Now we did not know where we were, whether we were Indians or British or what.

GLOSSARY

anna	one-sixteenth of a rupee; a rupee was worth 1/6 (7½p)
ashram	spiritual retreat
ayah	Indian nurse or nanny; lady's maid
Brahmin	the highest priestly caste among Hindus
char-wallah	tea-server or tea-boy
Dominion Status	term applied to the white dominions of Australia, Canada and New Zealand which were self-governing but which were linked to Britain through their recognition of the British Sovereign as their head of state
fakir	poor and needy; Muslim religious beggar. The British mistakenly used the word to describe a Hindu who had renounced his worldly possessions and dedicated himself to a solitary existence of meditation and prayer
Gandhiji	adding "ji" to the end of a person's name is a means of indicating affectionate and deep respect
Kaisar-i-Hind	Emperor or Empress of India
khadi	handspun cloth
ma-bap	mother and father
Maharaja	Great King; a Hindu prince
Mahatma	Great Soul
memsahib	lady, from "madam-sahib"
Muharram	the first month of the Muslim calendar which mourns the martyrdom of Husain, grandson of the prophet Muhammad, at the battle of Karbala in Persia (Iraq) in 680. Spanning ten days, the annual commemoration, which is celebrated particularly by Shi'ite Muslims, takes a variety of shapes including sermons, dancing bands, mourning rituals, as well as the building of model tombs (tazias) and their burial on the final day
munshi	interpreter; teacher of languages
Netaji	Leader
Pakistan	"Pak" in Urdu means "pure" and "stan" means "land", so "Pakistan" means "land of the pure". It is made from the letters of the Muslim-majority areas of north-west India: P for the Punjab, A for Afghania (the North-West Frontier Province), K for Kashmir, S for Sind and TAN for BaluchisTAN.
patwari	village accountant
purdah	veil or curtain; Muslim practice of keeping women in seclusion
Raj	kingdom; used in twentieth century chiefly to denote British rule in India from 1858 to 1947
Ramarajya	kingdom of King Rama whose story is told in the Ramayana, an epic Hindu poem supposedly composed as early as the fourth century B.C.
Satyagraha	"truth-force" or "soul-force"; force born of truth or non-violence
Swaraj	self-rule or self-government
tahsil	administrative unit of district
writer	clerk in the service of the East India Company

DATE LIST

1885	Indian National Congress established.
1905	Partition of Bengal.
1906	All-India Muslim League established.
1909	Indian Councils Act; separate electorate for Muslims introduced.
1911	Bengal reunited.
1915	Gandhi returns to India from South Africa.
1916	Lucknow Pact between Congress and Muslim League.
1917	Edwin Montagu, Secretary of State for India, announces that "the progressive realisation of responsible government as an integral part of the British Empire" is the goal of British policy in India.
1919	
April	Amritsar Massacre.
December	Government of India Act passed.
1920	Gandhi launches the non-cooperation movement.
1922	
February	Policemen murdered at Chauri Chaura; Gandhi suspends non-cooperation.
March	Gandhi arrested.
1927	Appointment of all-British Statutory Commission to review working of 1919 Act; proceedings boycotted by major Indian parties.
1928	Report by (Motilal) Nehru Committee, calling for Dominion Status and abolition of separate electorate, approved by All-Parties Convention.
1929	
October	Irwin's "Dominion Status" declaration.
December	Congress opts for civil disobedience to achieve complete independence.
1930	
March	Gandhi begins the salt march.
April	Gandhi breaks Salt Law.
May	Gandhi arrested.
November	First Round Table Conference meets in London.

1931	
February	Irwin and Gandhi begin peace talks.
March	Gandhi-Irwin Pact signed.
September	Gandhi attends second Round Table Conference in London.
1932	Resumption of civil disobedience; Gandhi and other Congress leaders arrested.
1933	Third and final Round Table Conference in London.
1934	Congress suspends civil disobedience; Jinnah returns to India to lead Muslim League.
1935	Government of India Act passed.
1937	Provincial elections; Congress rejects League proposals for coalition government in United Provinces.
1939	Congress governments in provinces resign; League observes "Deliverance Day".
1940	League meeting at Lahore approves "Pakistan" resolution.
1942	
March	Cripps Mission to India.
August	Congress launches "Quit India" movement.
1945	Labour Government elected in Britain.
1946	Cabinet Mission to India; League's call for Muslims to observe 16 August as "Direct Action Day" leads to Great Calcutta killing.
1947	
February	Prime Minister Attlee announces Britain's intention to leave India by June 1948.
March	Mountbatten becomes last Viceroy of India.
June	Indian leaders accept partition plan.
15 August	India and Pakistan become independent.
16 August	Award of Boundary Commission announced.
1948	
January	Gandhi assassinated by Hindu extremist.
February	Death of Jinnah.

BOOKS FOR FURTHER READING

General histories written for school use

Denis Judd, *The British Raj* (Wayland, London, n.d.)

B.N. Pandey, *The Rise of Modern India* (Hamish Hamilton, London, 1967)

Vishnu Prabhakar, *Story of Swarajya* (National Book Trust, New Delhi, 1971); *Swarajya* means self-rule

Elizabeth Mauchline Roberts, *Gandhi, Nehru and Modern India* (Methuen, London, 1974)

Richard Tames, *India and Pakistan in the Twentieth Century* (B.T. Batsford Ltd, London, 1980)

Malcolm Yapp, *The British Raj and Indian Nationalism* (Harrap, London, 1977)

Malcolm Yapp, *Gandhi* (Harrap, London, 1977)

The British in India

Charles Allen, *Plain Tales from the Raj* (André Deutsch, London, 1975)

Charles Allen, *Raj: A Scrapbook of British India 1877-1947* (André Deutsch, London, 1977)

Mark Bence-Jones, *The Viceroys of India* (Constable, London, 1982)

Roland Hunt and John Harrison (eds.), *The District Officer in India* (Scolar, London, 1980)

Nationalism, independence and partition

Subhas C. Bose, *The Indian Struggle 1920 – 1934* (Wishart, London, 1935)

Mohandas Karamchand Gandhi, *An Autobiography: The Story of my Experiments with Truth* (Jonathan Cape, London, 1949)

Stanley Wolpert, *Jinnah of Pakistan* (Oxford University Press, Oxford, 1985)

B.R. Nanda, *Mahatma Gandhi* (Allen & Unwin, London, 1958)

Jawaharlal Nehru, *Autobiography: Towards Freedom* (John Day, New York, 1941)

B.N. Pandey, *The Break Up of British India* (Macmillan, London, 1969)

B.N. Pandey, *Nehru* (Macmillan, London, 1976)

Kushwant Singh, *Train to Pakistan,* (Chatto & Windus, London, 1956)

Princely India

Charles Allen and Sharada Dwivedi, *Lives of the Indian Princes* (Century, London, 1984)

Clark Worswick, *Princely India* (Hamish Hamilton, London, 1980)

For Reference

Stephen Ashton and Penelope Tuson, *The India Library Office and Records: A Brief Guide for Teachers* (India Library Office and Records, London, 1985)

Patricia Bahree, *India, Pakistan and Bangladesh: A Handbook for Teachers* (External Division, School of Oriental and African Studies, University of London, 1982)

B.N. Pandey, *The Indian Nationalist Movement 1885-1947: Select Documents* (Macmillan, London, 1979)

Plain Tales from the Raj: A Catalogue of the BBC Recordings (India Office Library and Records and Imperial War Museum, London, 1981)

INDEX